UNLOCKING YOUR RENAISSANCE

Also, by Va'rai Unique

★ PLAYING LIFE TO WIN

The ultimate accountability journal

★ INHALE, EXHALE

Directions for a 14-day improvement of mental & physical health

Unlocking Your Renaissance

7 Keys to Transform Your Mindset & Inner Dialogue

by Va'rai Unique - CLF, CNLP, MBACP (Accred)

COPYRIGHT

COPYRIGHT

ISBN: 979-8-218-26197-9 | Hardback

ISBN: 979-8-990-15060-7 | Paperback

ISBN: 979-8-990-15061-4 | eBook & Kindle

Cover Design by Variety Elixir Branding Agency

Printed in the United States of America

Published by Variety Elixir Publishing

Variety Elixir Publishing offers their books at a discount for bulk purchases in the United States by corporations, institutions, and other organisations. For more information, please contact the Special Markets Department at the Variety Elixir Publishing company by emailing; bulksales@varietyelixir.com

LEGAL DISCLAIMER

The information provided in this self-help book is intended for general informational purposes only. The author and publisher of this book are not engaged in rendering legal, medical, financial, or professional advice. You should consult with a qualified professional for any legal, medical, financial, or professional concerns.

The author and publisher have made every effort to ensure the accuracy of the information herein. However, the author and publisher do not warrant or represent that the information provided in this book is complete, accurate, or up-to-date, and they disclaim all warranties, express or implied.

Any reliance you place on the information in this book is done at your own risk. The author and publisher shall not be liable for any special, incidental, consequential, or punitive damages arising from the use of, reliance on, or interpretation of the information provided.

The self-help techniques and strategies outlined in this book may not be suitable for every individual or situation. You should use your judgment and seek the advice of a qualified professional when applying any advice or techniques from this book to your own circumstances.

The names of individuals, organisations, products, and services mentioned in this book are purely for the purpose of providing examples and should not be considered endorsements. Any resemblance to actual persons, living or dead, events, or locales is entirely coincidental.

By reading this book, you agree to release and discharge the author, publisher, and any contributors from any and all claims or causes of action arising out of or in connection with the use of the information provided herein.

If you do not agree with these terms and conditions, you should not use or rely on the information in this book.

DEDICATION

I dedicate this book to my three beautiful children, David, My Wonderful Partner, Minister Francis, Ms. Napolitano, Mr. Rose & My Bonus Glam-Ma 'Grandma Collins' – Their presence in my life embodies abundance; their love not only nourishes but also serves as a remarkable wellspring of learning and personal growth.

I have also devoted this book for those with the tenacity to unlock the treasure in their heart so they can share within their sphere of influence and in-turn make the world a much richer place.

Agape xoxo

CONTENTS

Table of Contents

CONTENTS

Unlocking Your Renaissance

ACKNOWLEDGEMENTS

What started off as a simple journal, ended up as an incredible book. It was what felt right, but I couldn't do it without the help of certain individuals who I am grateful to have in my life.

First and foremost, I would like to thank my relationship with the creator of all things G-d. Special thanks to my both my parents who I have learnt to accept and love for who they're, to whom I thank for my existence. My best friend, who is a sister to me, she has loved me unconditionally throughout the decades of our friendship, a rare love I'm forever grateful for.

Special business thanks to Bev James, whom I had the pleasure of meeting through James Caan. She lit the NLP flame in life, and I become her first student at her academy, while also using her DISC app (which at the time was very future forward).

A huge thank you to Pastor Ron, from Westside Vineyard Church in sunny Los Angeles, your support and prayers mean a lot to me.

Also, a huge thank you to my first two mentors in business, who I met very early in my teenage era, while working at my first job at a local sports centre. You both helped me fully form my love for entrepreneurship when I suggested the creation of Camp Energy. You both believed in me, while everyone else said I was too young to complete such a huge task, yet I managed to execute the vision with your guidance.

My professors while studying at university for my BA Hons, I have finally taken your advice and become an author, thank you for the encouragement and seeing me as my authentic self before I did.

Thank you to every single human that I have encountered on my journey throughout my life, no matter the length of time, or whether deemed a good or bad experience, because in hindsight what some meant for my harm, has, and will always continue to be used for my good.

Applying the creative principles in this book, a portion of the proceeds will be used to Unlock the Renaissance for individuals who have experienced domestic violence within my hometown London (in the United Kingdom), New York & Los Angeles. Helping them rebuild and restore their lives. We want their hidden treasure to impact the world.

The organisations I have chosen to give back to, are non-profits I have had the pleasure of either working for and/or volunteered with for several years.

ACKNOWLEDGEMENTS

INTRODUCTION

Preparing for your Personal Renaissance

This is a breakthrough book and in the right hands it's very powerful. So, get ready to make your way towards the door of self-discovery and transformation. Within "Unlock Your Renaissance," is your keys to unlocking the incredible potential within you. It's a guide to reshape your mindset and harness the ultimate power of your inner dialogue to manifest positive change in your life.

In the grand theatre of life, your mindset and inner dialogue are the directors, scriptwriters, and lead actors. They shape your perceptions, influence your decisions, and ultimately determine the plot of your story. Yet, many of us underestimate the profound impact these internal forces have on our lives.

Think of your mindset as the lens through which you view the world. It colours every experience, every challenge, and every opportunity. Your inner dialogue, that constant conversation you have with yourself, is the narrator of your life's story. It can be your harshest critic or your most enthusiastic cheerleader. The good news is that you hold the pen to rewrite your script and redefine your character. You have the capability to reshape your frame of mind and reconstruct your inner dialogue to serve your highest aspirations and goals. This workbook is designed with neuro-linguistic programming exercises to be your partner on this remarkable metamorphosis.

Let's take a look at neuro-linguistic programming, which is often abbreviated as NLP. Developed by Richard Bandler and John Grinder, NLP is based on the premise that our thoughts, language, and behaviours are interconnected and can be influenced and fully adapted to achieve our desired outcomes. It is an effective psychological framework and a set of communication tools that can have a profound impact on our personal development. Here, I will give you a brief overview to explore what NLP is and why it is beneficial for shaping our mental state.

Understanding NLP

At its core, NLP is a versatile approach to understanding and changing human behaviour. It's founded on several key principles:

- Neurological Basis: The "neuro" in NLP refers to the idea that our experiences are processed through our senses and translated into neural representations in our minds. NLP recognizes that each person's subjective experience is unique, based on their perception of the world.

- Language is Key: The "linguistic" aspect highlights the significance of language in shaping our experiences. It emphasizes that the words we use to describe our experiences affect how we think and feel about them. NLP aims to improve communication and self-awareness through language.

- Programming for Change: The "programming" part focuses on our ability to reprogram our thought patterns and behaviours for positive change. NLP offers techniques to identify and transform limiting beliefs, habits, and negative thought processes.

Benefits for Mindsets

NLP has numerous benefits for shaping and enhancing our demeanour:

- Enhanced Self-Awareness: NLP encourages individuals to become more aware of their thoughts and thought patterns. This self-awareness is the first step toward personal growth and mindset modification.

- Improved Communication: Effective communication is a fundamental aspect of NLP. Learning NLP techniques can help individuals communicate more clearly, persuasively, and empathetically, which fosters better relationships and understanding.

- Mindset Reframing: One of the most powerful applications of NLP is its ability to reframe negative thought patterns. Through techniques like "submodalities" and "reframing," individuals can change how they perceive and react to specific situations, leading to more positive and growth-oriented thoughts.

- Goal Achievement: NLP offers tools for setting and achieving goals. By creating well-formed outcomes and utilizing strategies like the "well-formedness conditions," individuals can design a clear path to success.

- Emotional Intelligence: NLP enhances emotional intelligence by helping individuals better understand and manage their emotions. This is invaluable for improving relationships, reducing stress, and developing a resilient frame of mind.

- Overcoming Limiting Beliefs: NLP provides effective methods for identifying and challenging limiting beliefs. By doing so, individuals can break free from self-imposed mental constraints and foster a more empowering mindset.

- Effective Stress Management: NLP techniques such as "Anchoring" can help individuals manage stress and anxiety, allowing you to become more positive and relaxed.

- Boosting Confidence: NLP offers strategies for increasing self-confidence and self-esteem.

In conclusion, neuro-linguistic programming is a versatile and powerful tool for enhancing self-mastery. By understanding the interconnected nature of our thoughts, language, and behaviours, and by utilizing NLP techniques within this book, you will be able to reprogram your learned helplessness for greater self-awareness, improved communication, emotional intelligence, and ultimately, a more fulfilling and abundant life.

Now that we have had a brief introduction to NLP, let's take a deeper look at what we mean by renaissance. As we know life often unfolds as a series of chapters, each marked by its unique challenges and triumphs. Within this human experience, there comes a moment when you may find yourself in search of a personal renaissance—a profound rebirth of self, purpose, and passion. Just like the Renaissance period in history, where creativity, innovation, and a newfound appreciation for the arts flourished, your personal renaissance is a time of self-discovery and revitalization. It's a period where you rekindle your curiosity and embrace the desire to learn, grow, and explore.

Are you ready for a renaissance in your life? Can you feel the call to greater meaning in your life? Do you find yourself in a stagnant job, an exhausting daily routine, limiting relationships, or financial challenges? You might be going through significant life changes, such as divorce, relocation, or dealing with a loss in your family, or perhaps, you're finally ready to pursue a dream you've put off for too long. A personal transformation can take various forms, like deciding to start a business that you have thought about pursuing for years, or maybe you may be a stay-at-home parent who now would like to go back to work. Another may find their renaissance by deciding to travel abroad for the first time or taking your long-term relationship to the next level of marriage. Whatever it is that brings you to that place of rebirth, will also bring a beautiful new beginning. The process usually starts with a shedding, almost like the end of something. It is the feeling that comes from a deep unease, a restlessness even, that feeling that gets you questioning, 'I'm sure there is more to life than just this!'.

Do you sense a void in your life, an unsettling restlessness, or the inability to authentically express yourself? Perhaps you feel as if you've outgrown your current environment, no longer fitting in, and experiencing a sense of stagnation. If any of these statements resonate with you, it's a sign of experiencing creative discontent, and you may be primed for your very own transformative rebirth.

Regardless of what season in your life you may be in right now, your lack of inner peace is definitely an indication that your life is changing and if you embrace the change, you can begin the voyage to become your most authentic self. For hundreds of years, men and women around the world have known that creative discontent is the first stage of rebirth. That calling of something unknown, beckoning them to something greater within.

In the past, individuals, both men and women, served as sources of inspiration during the Renaissance era, a period marked by radical change. A time when sailors discovered lands afar, where different planets were discovered in the skies, to a time where we have advanced to modern day evolution. Renaissance men and women were not only pioneers of art, science, and innovation but were also deeply empowered by a profound sense of calling or vocation. This inner conviction fuelled their extraordinary contributions and transformative impact on society, marking an era where individuals pursued their passions and, in doing so, reshaped the course of history.

Consider Leonardo da Vinci, whose insatiable curiosity led him to excel in fields ranging from art to engineering. Similarly, Florence Nightingale's unwavering commitment to nursing marked a defining vocation, revolutionizing healthcare practices. Fast forward to today we can look at Elon Musk, who is a ground-breaking pioneer, reshaping industries through SpaceX, Tesla, and renewable energy companies. His relentless innovation is driving the future of technology and sustainability. These inspirational leaders, among many others, are remarkable examples of people that harnessed their inner callings to make unforgettable contributions that reshaped their respective sphere of influence and, in turn, the course of history. However, it is imperative to remember, personal renaissance is not limited to grand achievements but can manifest in various ways in one's life.

When we look at the current state of society, it appears that we are facing unparalleled issues, such as surging rates of depression, chronic anxiety, increasing isolation, and a pervasive lack of purpose. Many individuals today are struggling with a sense of powerlessness, often feeling helpless and doubting whether they can truly make a meaningful difference in our ever-changing society. There is no doubt that the renaissance men and women I referred to may have had such feelings, however they never allowed those feelings to cripple them, instead using them as a superpower to discover, create and elevate.

Today, even with the world of information at our fingertips, too often we allow ourselves to lose our inner knowing by not taking the time to do the shadow work, to look within, to ask ourselves the important sensitive questions we need to discover our authentic selves. This is why it is so common for many people to end up not knowing why or how they ended up where they currently are in life and have no clue how to get back on the right path.

As a certified life coach, who specializes in neuro-linguistic programming, I've seen too many people rush into life changing decisions without doing the much-needed inner work. One common example of rushing into life-changing decisions without doing the necessary inner work is a hasty marriage. Imagine a person who, after a brief courtship, impulsively decides to get married because they believe it will bring happiness and fulfilment. They might not have taken the time to understand their own emotional needs, values, or past relationship patterns.

The consequences of such a rushed decision can be negative. Once the honeymoon phase fades away, they may start to realize that they have fundamental differences in values or incompatible lifestyles. The lack of inner work and self-reflection can lead to feelings of dissatisfaction, disappointment, and conflict. This can result in the need for separation, divorce, or a long and emotionally challenging journey to rebuilding the relationship. This is probably why according to recent data in 2023, about 35-50% of first marriages end in divorce, while second marriages have a higher divorce rate of 60-70+%. Most divorces occur in the first five years of marriage, with communication problems, infidelity, and financial issues are the most common reasons for divorce.[1]

By not taking the time for inner work, individuals risk making life-changing decisions that are not aligned with their true selves, leading to unnecessary hardships and regrets. I have seen so many people from different backgrounds and career paths that are outwardly successful, to modern day societies standards, yet deep inside, they wrestle with the constant feeling that they have somehow misplaced a crucial piece of who they are. I have seen it time and time again with clients, friends and even throughout my career, where people have disregarded the importance of their own inner wisdom and ended up misguided.

As a result, we see it so often that men and women today end up going after what they think they should, instead of living out what they truly desire and are called to do. In contrast to the isolating and overwhelming nature of today's media, the foundational principles of Renaissance culture emphasize our inherent connection to the world, underscoring that every individual possesses the ability to effect meaningful change. In other words, the consequences of disregarding your inner wisdom results in delaying your calling if you're not already living in purpose.

A sense of change or calling can occur at any age, therefore it is never too late to discover your calling. When we discover our calling and live our authentic desires, we will feel a profound sense of fulfilment and happiness, as it aligns your actions with your innermost values and passions. This alignment will fuel an unwavering motivation and resilience, which will enable you to navigate past the obstacles you will face while the journey of 'becoming' with determination. Embracing your calling cultivates personal growth, encouraging continuous learning and development. It leads to you increasing your productivity and reduces your stress, as the work you're engaged in is rewarding. Your calling isn't just about the work you do; it's about living a life that's in harmony with who you were created to be.

Keep this in mind as you navigate through this workbook, as it's not just a passive reading experience; it's a dynamic tool for your personal growth journey. It's a place for reflection, self-assessment, and transformational exercises. It's your canvas to paint the masterpiece of your life with a mindset that empowers and an inner dialogue that uplifts. So, are you ready to take the first step toward unlocking your renaissance? Let's embark on this change together. Remember, the story of your life is still being written, and you have the power to make it a sensational one.

What You'll Discover

Throughout "Unlock Your Renaissance," you will embark on a voyage of self-discovery and empowerment. You will:

- Recognize Your Current Mindset: Gain insights into your existing mindset and uncover the beliefs that may be limiting your potential.

- Master Your Inner Dialogue: Learn techniques to become aware of your inner dialogue and how to shift it from self-doubt to self-affirmation.

- Cultivate a Growth Mindset: Embrace the power of a growth mindset, allowing you to see challenges as opportunities for growth and learning.

- Set Empowering Goals: Create a vision for your life and set actionable goals that align with your newfound mindset.

- Practice Positive Self-Talk: Develop habits of positive self-talk that reinforce your self-worth and potential.

- Overcome Limiting Beliefs: Learn strategies to challenge and overcome limiting beliefs that have held you back.

- Create an Action Plan: Develop a personalized action plan to implement the changes you desire in your life.

What you can expect

As you take your journey through this book, you may find yourself:

- Happier and more energetic

- Experiencing greater joy and more meaning in your day-to-day activities

- More aware of creative opportunities that actually align with who you were created to be

- More relaxed, joyful and open to new possibilities

- Notice that you are surrounded by supportive friends and mentors

- Able to embrace what inspires and energizes you

- Able to detect and reject the things and/or people that drain you

How to get the most from this book

To benefit from this book, you will need to:

- Get yourself a journal to record your journey
- Focus on one chapter at a time, doing the exercises and answering the questions throughout the book
- Checking in with the helpful reminders at the end.
- Be gentle with yourself. You will find the key to unlock new components of yourself is through joy, love and kindness. Stress, sadness or obligation will keep you locked out.
- Make sure you listen to yourself and recognize what energizes you and also stay alert to what drains you.
- Trust the process, trust yourself and your decisions, trust the creative power of the creator of the universe.

Now that you are as prepared as much as you can be to fully embrace your new future, let's begin to unlock your renaissance.

PART I

CREATING YOUR PERSONAL REBIRTH

PART I
CREATING YOUR PERSONAL REBIRTH

Key One | Recognising your Current Mindset & Talents

Your vision will become clear only when you can look into your own heart. Who looks outside dreams; who looks inside awakes.

Carl Yung

Now that you've realized you're prepared to embrace the next chapter in your life, what comes next? Your journey toward personal growth and transformation starts with a fundamental step: understanding where you currently stand in terms of your mindset. In this chapter, we will embark on the exploration of self-discovery, assessing your present mental landscape and navigating the path to make constructive shifts needed to embrace utilizing your new keys.

Self-reflection, the cornerstone of this transformative journey, is equivalent to gazing into a mirror—except this mirror reveals the intricate fabric of your thoughts, beliefs, and behaviours, unveiling the profound influence they hold over our lives. A conscious and candid appraisal of the predominant thoughts and attitudes that currently govern your life are as important as the air we breathe. Are they empowering or limiting? Optimistic or pessimistic? Reflect on the beliefs you currently possess about yourself, your capabilities, and your potential.

Further into the realm of self-discovery, we come to the notion of identifying our core values. When we complete these exercises, it compels us to peer deeply into our souls, exploring the very bedrock of our existence. What truly matters to you? The discovery of your core values is pivotal; it becomes a compass, guiding you toward happiness and fulfilment that your soul is truly desiring right now. Now this will require you to be honest with yourself and sometimes you will find that it will make you uncomfortable and reactive but be gentle with yourself. Sometimes you will discover that you have lost touch with your true values.

That was Daniels experience, even though he was a diligent and ambitious individual, known for his unwavering commitment to self-improvement through his experience of personal NLP coaching with me, when it came to reviewing his current frame of mind, he was undeniably shocked with the results that rose to the surface. When our session began, Daniel opened up about his aspirations and dreams. He spoke earnestly about the values he had held dear for many years, values that had driven him towards the many successes in his career. The session was intended to be a moment of self-discovery, a chance to reaffirm his beliefs. However, as the coaching session delved deeper, Daniel was taken aback by what he discovered. He realised that some of the values he had cherished and lived by were now misaligned with his authentic self. The shock of this revelation was both profound and unsettling. It felt like the foundation of his identity was literally crumbling beneath him.

Over the course of the session, he couldn't help but reflect on the consequences of these misaligned values. He recognised that they had led him to take a competitive and often ruthless approach in his work. While he had been praised for his dedication, he had sometimes acted insensitively and even inconsiderately toward his colleagues. His whole demeanour had changed and the way he started speaking to me was with such force and attitude, thankfully I was fully aware that he was projecting, so I allowed him to fully be in that moment. As the coaching session concluded, the storm of emotions that raged within Daniel throughout the session just erupted. He felt really angry with himself for not realising these misaligned values earlier on. His disappointment and frustration for only discovering this within a coaching session began to consume him, and he was unable to find the self-compassion he needed to navigate this moment of reckoning. I reminded him that it was okay to feel these emotions and to let them be expressed while in an environment that was safe for him to do so.

He needed to be gentle with himself, but in the days that followed, instead of approaching his newfound self-awareness with the gentleness and understanding he deserved, Daniel took out his frustration on some

18

of his colleagues. He became so short-tempered, critical, and unsympathetic towards their ideas and opinions. He mistakenly believed that by being more assertive, he could regain his sense of control, but really it was his ego screaming to be heard.

His colleagues were totally taken back and bewildered by this sudden change in behaviour, unable to fully grasp why Daniel was acting so harshly all of a sudden. His once harmonious work environment had turned into a tense and uncomfortable one. However, it didn't take long for Daniel to realise the toll his behaviour was taking, not just on himself but also within his professional relationships. He recognised that he was repeating the same mistakes he had previously uncovered in his coaching session—acting without empathy and disregarding the feelings of others.

After much contemplation, he decided to have an additional coaching session, as he needed to discuss his reactions. Daniel shared his recent experiences while at work and the realizations that had triggered his turbulent behaviour. I encouraged him to be kinder to himself, to recognize that self-discovery often brings a lot of discomfort, but that this discomfort was the first key to unlocking his personal renaissance.

After the session Daniel embraced his current situation by beginning to heal the rifts in his professional relationships. He spoke to his colleagues and apologized for his behaviour and explained the journey of self-discovery he had been on. He also promised himself while in one of our subsequent sessions that he would make sure he saw the process through on aligning his values with his actions, this time being more compassionate both to himself and to all those around him.

In the end, Daniel's story became the first step and also a testament to the power of self-awareness and self-compassion. His journey from self-discovery to redemption taught him that understanding and embracing one's true values required patience, gentleness, and the courage to admit one's imperfections.

We have all been where Daniel has been, and as we delve into self-reflection, we have to welcome that inevitably we will unearth some self-limiting beliefs. These are the insidious doubts that creep in, casting shadows on our capabilities and full potential. They manifest as persistent negative self-talk, fears of inadequacy, and scepticism about the tasks we need to undertake to get to the places we seek to be.

The emotional landscape, too, warrants your exploration. Are you frequently burdened by stress, plagued by anxiety, or haunted by unhappiness? An intimate understanding of your emotional patterns offers an invaluable map to pinpoint the areas where positive change is most needed. Do they align with your authentic passions and aspirations? Or have they been crafted under the influence of external expectations and societal norms?

It's so imperative to ensure that your aspirations are a reflection of your true self, free from the constraints of conformity, so that we are not caught up in the endless round of responsibilities, and feeling like life is just an upward battle. You will not find the keys to your renaissance by feeling burdened, you will only feel it with truth, honest and pure love, and joy.

Italian Renaissance artists and philosophers perceived love as the creative force of the cosmos. Similarly, in your own life, being forthright with your current state and then rediscovering your passions will infuse you with the profound delight of exploration.

Happiness & Talent

What makes you really happy? What is your passion? What do you love to do? In the hustle and bustle of daily life, countless individuals have drifted away from their once-vibrant dreams. This was precisely Maria's reality, who lived with her husband John and their three children.

Their home was filled with love and laughter, yet Maria couldn't help but feel a deep void within her. It was as if her vibrant spirit had been dimmed by the routines of daily life, and she had lost the spark that once defined her.

You see, before the responsibilities of marriage and motherhood, Maria had been a passionate and talented athlete. Her dream was to become a professional athlete, and she had been well on her way to making it a reality. But as life had unfolded, she met John, fell in love, and they soon started a family. Maria's athletic dreams were pushed to the background as she embraced her role as a wife and mother. She became deeply entwined in the day-to-day routines of caring for her family, and her own aspirations had slowly faded away.

One morning, while preparing breakfast for her family, Maria looked in the mirror and noticed the same glimmer in her eyes that once burned brightly had dimmed. She missed the thrill of her athletic pursuits and realized she had let her own passions slip away. One evening, after a heartfelt conversation with John, Maria decided it was time to reclaim her lost dreams. With John's unwavering support, they worked out a plan to balance her family responsibilities with her yearning for athletic achievement. Maria began by dedicating time to training and pursuing her athletic passions once more. John shared the household duties, ensuring that Maria had the freedom to chase her long-lost dream. Together, they committed to this new journey of self-discovery.

The transformation in Maria was remarkable. Her laughter returned, and her eyes sparkled with the determination to chase her dream once again. She retraced the path she had once walked, realizing that while she might not become a professional athlete, she found genuine happiness in pursuing her passion, with her family cheering her on every step of the way. As Maria pursued her athletic dreams with unwavering passion, her family shared in the joy of her accomplishments, uniting in a thrilling journey of achievement together. Her children witnessed her unwavering dedication, and her husband proudly stood by her side, rekindling their own desires and dreams along the way.

Maria's journey wasn't just about recapturing her lost passions; it was about proving to herself and her family that dreams could be pursued at any stage of life. Her story became an inspiration to her friends and family, reminding everyone that it's never too late to rediscover one's true self and chase one's dreams, no matter where life's journey had taken them. Maria's life was now a testament to the enduring power of pursuing one's passions, and her home was filled with not only love and laughter but the fulfilment that comes with living authentically.

Realizing your joys is comparable to discovering a treasury within your own heart. It's the profound awareness of those activities, experiences, and moments that light up your soul. These joys are the emotions and sensations that make life meaningful and memorable.

Finding your joys is a deeply personal journey. It's about recognizing what stirs your passion, what brings a genuine smile to your face, and what makes your heart race with excitement. These joys might come from pursuing a creative hobby, spending time with loved ones, exploring new places, achieving personal goals, or simply savouring the beauty of everyday life.

When you realize your joys, you connect with a profound sense of contentment and purpose. It's like finding your own unique rhythm in the symphony of life. These joys become your guiding stars, illuminating the path to a more fulfilling existence. In addition, acknowledging your joys can have a transformative impact on your overall well-being. Engaging in activities that bring you happiness not only reduces stress but also enhances your mental and emotional resilience. It's a source of motivation and inspiration, driving you to reach new heights and embrace life's challenges with a positive mindset. Your joys are a powerful source of energy and vitality, a reminder that life is not merely a journey but a celebration. Embracing them is an affirmation that you are living authentically, in alignment with your true self. So, take the time to explore, discover, and realize your joys, for they are the keys to a richer and more fulfilling life.

Going Back to Move Forward

I'm sure you have heard the phrase "hindsight is better than foresight". Ultimately this means that sometimes it is more beneficial for us to look at the past to help us with the future. So, let's take it all the way back to our early escapes. Think of times when you would get lost in an activity, maybe as early as when you were a child; a long time ago in Wisconsin, a young boy named Frank Lloyd Wright spent his childhood days exploring the natural world that surrounded him. Little did anyone know that this child's keen eye for design and his unyielding curiosity would lead him to become one of the most influential architects in history.

From a very early age, Frank displayed an innate talent for envisioning structures that harmonized with their surroundings. His favourite pastime was sketching the landscapes, wildlife, and buildings he encountered in the charming valley of Spring Green. His Mother soon recognized his exceptional ability and encouraged him to explore his artistic inclinations. As he grew older, Frank's artistic prowess continued to flourish. He attended engineering school and began working in architecture, but his passion for designing buildings that integrated with nature never waned. He realized that his true calling lay in creating structures that not only served a functional purpose but also celebrated the beauty of their surroundings.

Frank's journey to becoming an architect was not without its challenges. He faced opposition from those who adhered to conventional architectural norms. However, his unwavering dedication to his childhood passions and unique vision eventually led him to forge a new path in the field of architecture. Over the years, Frank Lloyd Wright's talent blossomed, and he designed iconic buildings like Fallingwater and the Guggenheim Museum. His designs, known for their organic architecture, became revered worldwide.

Frank's story is a testament to the power of nurturing childhood talents and passions. His relentless pursuit of innovative architecture, driven by his innate gift, left an indelible mark on the world. It truly reminds us that the dreams and talents of our youth can lead to radical achievements and shape the course of history.

What was true for Frank is true for you today. Discovering and using your gifts will bring you pure joy, and powerful creative energy, that will illuminate the path to your calling. There are so many stories from Renaissance days to modern times, where artists, scientists, saints, and scholars discovered their gifts, which led them to their true callings and with each story an undeniable pattern arises; the vast majority discovered their gifts while they were children. I'm very aware that I mention people who are well known legends, that have impacted the world, but please do not diminish your calling as a result because each person in this world holds significance, each person contributes uniquely, and each person leaves impact when in alignment with their calling.

If you struggle to pinpoint a passion that deeply captivates you, I suggest revisiting your childhood memories. Our inner child, with its innate wonder and curiosity, persists within us, despite the added responsibilities of adulthood. When you remember the activities that you enjoyed, make a note of them in a notebook. This will be a valuable tool

25

for your inner reflective journey. Remember as we discover our keys, there are exercises to complete at the end of each chapter. Not to be taken lightly, these exercises will be the catalyst to aiding your transformation.

⇒ Key One Mindset Exercise ⇐

Let's take some time to review our mindset and talents. Set aside around thirty to sixty minutes, preferably in a quiet place when you could be alone, so you're not interrupted. Make sure you take your notepad, so that you can jot down your thoughts and memories, while answering the following questions about your current mindset;

- What are my core beliefs about myself, my abilities, and potential?
- What truly matters to me in life?
- What are my core values and principles?
- Do I hold any self-limiting beliefs, and if so, what are they?
- How do I react to challenging situations and setbacks?
- What is my true passion, and do I pursue it?
- What are my most significant strengths and areas for improvement?
- How do I approach change and adapt to new circumstances?
- Do I set and work towards specific goals in my life?
- Am I satisfied with my current state of mind and overall well-being?

When you have finished with these questions, take some time to process what you have discovered, and then when you feel ready to move on, we will do a NLP exercise that I like to call Belief Rewiring, when completed repetitively it will reframe your limiting beliefs that you discovered in the earlier exercise and replace them with empowering ones, through visualization and emotional association. Regular practice can lead to a positive shift in your thought patterns and behaviours very quickly.

Belief Rewiring Steps

Identify Limiting Beliefs: Start by identifying a specific limiting belief that you want to reframe. It could be related to self-doubt, fear, or any negative thought pattern that holds you back.

1. Clear Your Mind: Find a quiet and comfortable space, sit down, and close your eyes. Take a few deep breaths to clear your mind.

2. Visualize the Belief: In your mind's eye, visualize the limiting belief as an object or image. Make it as clear as possible.

3. Associate Emotions: As you visualize this belief, connect it with the emotions you typically feel when this belief is triggered. Feel those emotions as vividly as you can.

4. Replace the Belief: Now, visualize another image or object that represents an empowering and positive belief that you want to

adopt. This should be the opposite or a reframing of your limiting belief.

5. Associate Positive Emotions: As you focus on the new belief, associate it with positive emotions. Feel the confidence, joy, and empowerment it brings.

6. Swap the Images: Imagine taking the image of the limiting belief and gradually replace it with the image of the empowering belief. As you do this, feel the positive emotions growing stronger.

7. Repeat the Process: Repeat this exercise as often as needed to reinforce the new belief and weaken the old one.

8. Action Plan: After the exercise, create an action plan to put your new belief into practice. Take small steps aligned with this belief to solidify the change in your mindset.

With your new perspective now is the time to reflect on the joys of your pastimes. Take a deep breath, close your eyes, and make sure you're completely relaxed. Allow your thoughts to drift back to a significant childhood memory. Regardless of your family background, reminisce about those moments when you discovered solace, optimism, and a newfound sense of self filled with joy. As a child, my friend Danielle found that playing dress up in her mother's clothes and also making items around the house into clothes really made her happy. When we used to play together, she would find a way to dress me up to, tucking and folding towels, scarfs, you name it, she used it. Today she is a renowned stylist to celebrities worldwide, making them look amazing.

Once you've recaptured your personal memory of happiness and inner strength as a child, jot down your responses to the following questions regarding that memory;

- How did I spend my time?
- What did I love to do?
- What did I look & feel like while taking part in this activity?
- What did my family and/or teachers say I was good at?
- When I was a child, what were my top five things to do, where I just lost track of time?
- What was I always curious about and do really well?
- What were all my favourite accomplishments as a child?

⇒ Key One Gifts & Talents Reflection ⇐

Reflect on your gifts and talents, jot down your insights, and celebrate your journey of exploring your mindset and abilities while taking positive action, with the questions on the next page:

1. What choices currently no longer appeal to you?
2. What choices attract you?
3. How can you use your gifts in this new season?
4. Were there any gifts on your lit that shocked you?
5. Are there any gifts on your list that you have done since you were a child?

6. Pick your top three and ask yourself "How can I use these three gifts over the course of the next week?" (for example, if you enjoy dancing, check if there is a dance class nearby, or look on YouTube for dance sessions you could do at home).

Time to move on to the next key, to unlock your Renaissance journey.

PART I

Key Two | Opening the Inner Journey: Embracing Heartfelt Values

To be yourself in a world that is constantly trying to make you something else is the greatest accomplishment.

Ralph Waldo Emerson

Now that you have uncovered your talents and gifts, this chapter will assist you in detachment and carving out additional time to fully utilize your gifts fully. We will also take a deep dive into our values, as they develop our character, and it's our character that creates our fortune. But one step at a time, as first our path to unlocking that door involves decluttering distractions and shedding energy-draining elements that will hinder our progress.

Like the majority of people in this day and age, Janiya spent most of her time at work. As the director of a dynamic public relations company, she was constantly busy with strategically planning the brand identity of her clients, while continually dismissing herself. After enduring long workdays, she would hastily prepare a salad, followed by dressing up at home for the celebrity events hosted by her firm, which often extended late into the night. Once the weekend would come around, she would be at the daytime events for the agency, overseeing the event staff and making sure everything was in order. Janiya took this job after relocating from another state, determined to fill the void of leaving her friends and family behind, while looking for a fresh start. Trying to fill the loneliness, she constantly fills her days with more work, making sure her days were full. But now the constant pressure made her feel like her life was unruly and unmanageable.

People who are workaholics, like Janiya are driven by adrenaline, and anxiety. When you're constantly on the go and under so much pressure, your creativity and joy is buried by the continuous stress and exhaustion, which weakens our memory and undermines our health. It causes the overuse of mediators that switch the stress response on and off. This accumulation of stress is known as 'allostatic load' and can adversely affect the brain.[2] Another term we all know of too describe this state of mind is fight or flight, which can serve us well in an emergency, but when you constantly exert adrenaline, cortisol and norepinephrine to prepare the body for physical action it results in poor health, really bad judgement and a real miserable quality of life.

Have you been living life like it's a constant emergency? If Janiya's story sounds familiar to you, you can stop your own frenzied cycle by re-shifting your inner life. By clearing away your mental clutter, you will revive your intuition and your implicit memory, a term psychologists use to describe tapping into your unconscious awareness, the place where wisdom and insight resides within us. Many of the greats you know, dating back to the renaissance have used this reservoir of knowledge to release their full potential.

In this Chapter, you'll begin to listen to yourself on a deeper level, releasing what is blocking you from being your authentic self. We will start with the art of detachment, which will help you with the unlock the door of liberation. Detachment, in this context, does not mean indifference or disconnection from the world. Instead, it refers to the ability to maintain an objective perspective, to separate ourselves from the noise and chaos that often surrounds us. It is about clearing the path of distractions and doubts, allowing us to focus on our gifts and talents, and how we can best utilize them. It's when you take the take the time to detach, focusing on your inner self, it becomes easier for you to bring your full potential back to life.

In the heart of 19th century China, where ancient traditions held sway, there lived a remarkable woman named Cixi, who had fire in her soul. Her journey, one of courage and audacity, would see her rise from a lowly background to the highest echelons of power.

Cixi was born in 1835, a time when China was ruled by the Qing Dynasty, a society that demanded her silence and submission, Cixi refused

34

to play by those rules. Her humble beginnings in a Manchu family offered no hint of the extraordinary destiny that awaited her. However, fate had other plans. At the tender age of 16, she was chosen as one of Emperor Xianfeng's concubines, an honour that would drastically alter the course of her life.

But life within the palace was far from the fairy tale Cixi might have imagined. She encountered a world of fierce competition, a constant struggle for favour and influence. The palace was a place of intrigue, where power struggles played out behind its ornate walls.

Yet Cixi possessed an inner wisdom that set her apart. She cultivated the virtue of detachment, a skill that would serve her well in the turbulent years ahead. She observed, she listened, and she learned. Over time, her wisdom grew, and she began to make her mark.

Tragedy struck in 1861 when Emperor Xianfeng passed away, leaving the empire in a state of chaos. It was then that Cixi, with her unparalleled insight, took action. She staged a coup to protect her young son's right to the throne, a move that was highly unorthodox at the time. Her courage and determination were on full display as she navigated the treacherous waters of imperial politics.

As she rose to power, Cixi combined her wisdom of detachment with her unwavering dedication to her vocation. She was determined to bring China into the modern era, to save it from the encroaching forces of colonialism and internal strife. With fearless resolve, she implemented a series of reforms that touched every aspect of Chinese society, from education to industry.

Cixi's reign marked a turning point in China's history. She modernized the country's infrastructure, embraced technological advancements, and championed women's rights. Her legacy lives on in the vast transformation she set in motion, a testament to her remarkable courage and vision.

Empress Dowager cixi's journey is a tale of a woman who defied the odds, combined her wisdom of detachment with the courage to be herself, and changed the course of history. Her courage and resilience in the face of immense challenges transformed her from a concubine into the ruler who would launch modern China. Her story is a testament to the enduring power of vision, determination, and audacity in the face of adversity. Her legacy as a leader, reformer, and visionary continues to inspire, reminding us that even in the face of immense challenges, courage and wisdom can pave the way to a brighter future.[3]

Detachment and Courage

While our lives may not be as eventful as Empress Dowager Cixi's, embracing your true calling always entails a courageous journey. It involves looking beyond societal norms, recognizing your talents, embracing your individuality, and becoming the person you are destined to be. Research has shown that people with resilience, which is the ability to overcome challenges, and who also have positive emotions, achieve excellence, and also have powerful inner lives.[4]

A period of required isolation focuses attention, with laser-like precision, channelling one's thoughts and energy. In the midst of her secluded life in the forbidden city, Empress Dowager Cixi found moments of solitude that allowed her to reflect on her talents and purpose. These interludes offered her a unique opportunity for introspection. Away from the bustling court, she contemplated her responsibilities and began to recognize her potential for change and reform. This enforced detachment gave her the space she needed to assess her calling and gather the courage to act upon it, ultimately influencing China's history. Throughout the course of history, individuals have, in times of crisis, grown to embrace the core values residing within their hearts.

In our own time, Malala Yousafzai, a resident of Pakistan's Swat Valley, championed girls' education in defiance of Taliban restrictions. She was targeted by the Taliban, who boarded her school bus and shot her in the head. Miraculously, she survived the attack, and persevered. Her story of courage and resilience transformed her into a global symbol for girls' education. At 17, she became the youngest Nobel Prize laureate. Malala's journey remains an inspiration for all.

Any major change in life can bring you to a place of detachment and a new perspective. This can range from ending a relationship, relocating to another town or country, or even a change of career. Detachment is a journey from the familiar world into one of rejuvenation, echoing the rites of passage: separation, initiation, and integration. This wisdom grants you enhanced clarity, authenticity in action, and the ability to fully embrace your creative, courageous self. Sometimes however we get distracted from accessing this inner wisdom that comes with detachment, or even worse, doubt or sometimes distractions will creep in.

Distractions come in many forms - from the constant buzz of social media notifications to the demands of our daily lives. These distractions can easily pull us away from our path, diverting our attention and energy from our true passions and talents. To combat this, we must practice mindfulness, being fully present in each moment. This allows us to recognize distractions for what they are and choose not to engage with them.

Let's consider the example of John, a talented musician. John had a gift for creating beautiful melodies, but he found himself constantly distracted by his day job, social media, and the demands of his social life. These distractions pulled him away from his music, leaving him feeling frustrated and unfulfilled. It was only when he began practicing mindfulness that he was able to recognize these distractions and choose not to engage with them. He set aside specific times for his music, turned off his social media notifications, and learned to say no to social engagements that did not serve his passion. This allowed him to focus on his music, to explore and develop his talent, and to find joy in his gift.

Doubt, on the other hand, is a more insidious obstacle. It creeps into our minds, questioning our abilities and undermining our confidence. Doubt can make us second-guess our talents and question whether we are truly capable of achieving our goals. To overcome doubt, we must cultivate self-belief and confidence. This involves acknowledging our achievements, no matter how small, and reminding ourselves of our capabilities.

For instance, consider the story of Lisa, a gifted writer. Lisa had always loved writing, but she was plagued by doubt. While she would take time out to sit still and write, she would question whether her writing was good enough, whether she could ever be successful, and whether her work was worth sharing with the world. This doubt held her back, preventing her from fully embracing her talent. It was only when she began to cultivate self-belief that she was able to overcome her doubt. She started by acknowledging her achievements, celebrating each story she completed, each positive feedback she received. She reminded herself of her passion for writing and her ability to create compelling narratives. This helped her to build confidence in her talent, allowing her to share her work with the world and to find fulfilment in her writing.

Once we have cleared the path of distractions and doubts, we can truly focus on our gifts and talents. We can explore them, develop them, and find ways to share them with the world. This is when we truly start to thrive, to live a life that is authentic and fulfilling.

Remember, the journey of self-discovery is not a straight path. It is a winding road filled with challenges and obstacles. But with detachment, mindfulness, and self-belief, we can navigate this road with grace and resilience. We can clear the path of distractions and doubts, allowing our gifts and talents to shine brightly. The stories of Empress Dowager Cixi, John and Lisa serve as reminders of what we can achieve when we learn to detach from distractions and doubts and focus on our unique gifts and talents.

Methods of Detachment

You can achieve increased detachment by stepping away from your usual daily patterns. A few methods to accomplish this include:

- Meditation and Mindfulness: Dedicate time each day to meditate or practice mindfulness to quiet your mind and increase self-awareness. It doesn't have to be for an extended amount of time, a simple 10-15 minutes can make a huge difference.

- Nature Retreats: Spend time in nature by taking hiking trips, or simply going for long walks in the outdoors. Aim for once a week, just to make a start.

- Digital Detox: Reduce screen time by unplugging from electronic devices, including social media and emails, for a specific period. Whether daily for an hour, or periodically for an extended period of time, for example monthly for a whole weekend.

- Travel: Explore new places, cultures, and environments, even if it's just a short weekend getaway or even a staycation in town, but in a nice hotel.

- Artistic Expression: Engage in creative activities such as painting, writing, or playing music, which can help you express your emotions and thoughts differently.

- Physical Activities: Participate in physical activities like yoga, sports, or fitness routines that allow you to disconnect from your daily concerns. This does wonders for your mind and your body.

- Reading: Delve into a good book that transports you to different worlds and perspectives, but helps you learn something new.

- Spend Time Alone: Set aside moments to be by yourself, reflecting on your thoughts and feelings without external distractions. This could be in your local park, sitting on your balcony, or visiting the local library.

- Attend Retreats: Consider participating in a retreat where you can spend a few days in a quiet and natural setting.

Each of these methods can provide an opportunity to detach from your routine and gain a fresh perspective on life.

Dennis, a pharmacist in London, has a great source of creativity. Every Saturday he carves times out to be contemplative, with his renaissance notebook. He takes time to leave behind the woes of work and his household responsibilities, he heads out to his favourite quiet pub, and reflects on his life. The time he invests in contemplative afternoons brings him abundant rewards: A broader outlook on life, innovative ideas, and creative resolutions to present challenges. When the day concludes, Dennis returns home with a sense of tranquillity, poised to embrace the following workday enriched by the insights of detachment.

At first some of my clients cannot fathom taking time out to detach. Their schedules are packed full with commitments, and distractions, that fill up their lives, taking them away from tapping into their authentic selves. Are any of these diversions recognizable to you?

- ❖ Constant pressure
- ❖ Too much to do
- ❖ Scrolling on the internet
- ❖ Cluttered household
- ❖ Continual interruptions
- ❖ Filling time with the television
- ❖ Mindless socializing
- ❖ A gossiper or complainer in your life
- ❖ Taking on other people's demands
- ❖ Interruptions from electronics
- ❖ Or something else?

For now, just write a list of your personal distractions and also any activities that are draining, in your notebook. Be completely honest with yourself while writing your list. We will learn how to deal with all of them at the end of this key chapter. But first ask yourself; is there an energy drain in your life? Maybe this story resonates with you?

Nick and Vera had a tradition of having lunch together during their church entertainment team breaks and occasionally a phone call midweek to go other their teamwork, however Nick would always end up venting and gossiping about everyone, blaming others for life's problems. However, Vera felt really drained, and always ended up with headaches after they would speak, making her realize she needed to reclaim her life's balance. Despite Nick finding solace in Vera's listening, encouragement, and prayers, she decided that it was time to focus on the teamwork for church, amongst her own personal projects that she had. She sent Nick a text message, explaining that their usual Sunday lunches together would be coming to a halt, as she needed time alone to focus on her work, but offered a midweek text for checking in when time permitted.

One small change can make a huge difference. Vera's single lunch dates had relieved her stress and breathed new life into her energy levels. Without the constant energy draining conversations with Nick, her headaches had disappeared, her projects were completed, and she had a fresh outlook on life.

To bring greater balance in your life, choose one of the previous detachment exercises. Don't wait for everything to be perfect to make the first step, start immediately and watch what happens. If you start now, you will reach your desired goal quicker. Remember the famous Chinese proverb stating that 'a journey of a thousand miles begins with a single step.'[5]

As you start to eradicate all your draining activities, you may start to feel like you're not sure what to do with yourself. The constant hustle and noise in your life may not have brought fulfilment, but they did provide a rush of adrenaline, excitement, and activity. Simplifying can initially be disorienting until you become accustomed to your natural pace. If you find yourself feeling restless, take a moment to reflect on what you genuinely want. Tune in to your body's signals and consider if relaxation is what you may truly need at this time. Explore how to make the most of your newfound time without reverting to old routines. Prioritize self-care and creative use of your time.

⇒ Mini Mindful Detachment Exercise ⇐

This quick NLP activity can help you detach briefly and regain composure during busy days.

- Find a Quiet Space: Take a brief break in a quiet and comfortable place.

- Seat and Breathe: Sit comfortably, close your eyes if desired, and take three slow, deep breaths.

- Visualize Serenity: Imagine a peaceful place, like a serene beach or a tranquil garden. Picture yourself there, absorbing the calmness.

- Positive Affirmation: Repeat a simple, positive affirmation silently. For example, "I am at peace" or "I am in control."

- Focus on Breath: Concentrate on your breath for a minute, allowing stress to melt away with each exhale.

- Return Refreshed: Open your eyes and return to your tasks with a sense of renewal and detachment.

Now would be a great time to review your unmet needs, so you can understand yourself better. It's a good idea to make sure that you are very honest with yourself when making this list.

Simplify your life by doing the following (in no order):

- ❖ Go on a gradual media diet.
- ❖ Avoid any temptations you may have.
- ❖ Stop comparing yourself to others.
- ❖ Slow down and go at a natural pace.
- ❖ Stop doing activities that you have outgrown.
- ❖ Immediately remove people who drain your energy.
- ❖ Declutter your primary place, whether it's your home and/or office.

It may feel alien to you at first when applying the above simplifications, but like any tool, the more you use it, the better it serves you.

⇒ **Key Two Questions** ⇐

Once you have simplified your life gradually, ask yourself the following:

1. What patterns do I need to break?
2. What do I want to do with my new free time?
3. What unmet needs do I need to nurture?
4. What are some healthy ways I can meet my needs?
5. Are there any other areas I can remove distractions, and if so, where?

6. How can I use my gifts more now?

7. How can I listen and follow my heart more?

Record your insights to unlock your renaissance in your notebook.

Time to Celebrate Yourself

As you move forward with finding your keys to unlocking your Renaissance, it's important to see how far you have come. Some of you will see immediate breakthroughs, while others may have results at a slower pace. Either way, it is imperative that you see all victories as such, even if it's as small as detaching from a major distraction, going for a new daily walk, or simply following the prompts in this book. Every step is drawing you closer to your desired outcome. The results may not be clear yet, but you are doing your part.

With each victory, don't wait for external recognition. Your new Renaissance begins right now as soon as you took the first step in finding the keys to unlock your new beginning. Celebrate as you go along, as gratitude is a powerful tool to helping you on this journey. How you celebrate, is up to you, it could be treating yourself to your favourite chocolate bar or treat yourself to lunch. Choose something that you enjoy and celebrate at each stage.

When you're taking on a huge task, breaking it into manageable bite size goals makes it more digestible. After each major milestone, taking time to celebrate will strengthen your commitment to finishing, while energizing and motivating you, one celebration at a time. This is how I finished this book, one celebration at a time, reminding myself that small and steady wins the race.

As you begin to live more authentically, you may be stunned at the changes, and people around you may also notice. Don't worry about those that complain to you, and my make comments like "You've changed", yet as you continue to embrace this new lease of life, and indulge in your newfound happiness, your original authenticity will hold such a power over you, you won't want to let go.

⇒ Key Two Detachment Reminders ⇐

- ✓ Detach from the noisy world around you.
- ✓ Get rid of unnecessary distractions.
- ✓ Make time to complete activities that you love.
- ✓ Create quality time for yourself.
- ✓ Less is more. SLOW DOWN when you need it most.

Embracing Heartfelt Values

When we are out of touch with our true values, we cannot function at our best, amidst the repetitive routines and the influence of external factors, impulsive behaviours, and desires, we find ourselves. However, as we confirm our core values, our lives are ignited by our most profound convictions. Empress Dowager Cixi's values helped her become one of the greatest leaders in the world. Like Cixi, you, too, possess guiding values that can infuse your life with purpose.[6]

Our Longing for Purpose

Meaning and purpose are the cornerstones of a fulfilling and well-lived life. They provide us with a sense of direction, a reason to strive, and the motivation to face life's challenges with resilience. Numerous studies have highlighted the crucial role of meaning in human existence, showing that individuals who have a strong sense of purpose tend to be healthier, happier, and more resilient in the face of adversity. Moreover, a life without meaning has been linked to higher rates of depression, anxiety, and overall dissatisfaction. It is through meaningful pursuits that we find a deeper connection to our true selves, others, and the world. Without meaning, life can feel empty and futile. Therefore, the pursuit of meaning and purpose isn't just a desirable aspect of human existence; it's a fundamental need that enriches our lives, enhances our well-being, and contributes to our overall happiness and contentment.

As psychiatrist Carl Yung realized, without meaning, people get stuck in emotional distress. He believed that a lack of meaning, and purpose could lead to contributing to a sense of inner emptiness and despair. Jung's work in psychology, particularly in the realm of individual growth and self-realization, underscored the significance of meaning and purpose for human well-being. Jung's ideas and observations have had a lasting impact on the field of psychology, and many studies have explored concepts related to Jungian psychology, archetypes, personality types, and individuation. His work continues to influence and inspire researchers and practitioners in various psychological fields. Confirming that as we meet today's challenges with courage and resourcefulness, we must completely believe that what we do matters, that our actions, when aligned with our true values and desires, are part of a larger pattern of meaning.

In the pursuit of a fulfilling life, understanding and embracing our values is paramount. Our values are the compass that guides us, the foundation upon which we build our lives. They are the principles that define who we are and what we stand for. Living in alignment with our values allows us to live with heart and meaning, to lead a life that is authentic and fulfilling.

Harnessing the Power of Inner Drive

When you follow your true values, your inner drive will give you the motivation that comes from within, to engage in the activities that will lead to higher levels of engagement, performance, and satisfaction. This will lead you to joy and fulfilment. However, when you do the opposite of this, and base your self-worth on other people's approvals, or societies norms, you will multiply chronic stress, anxiety, and compulsive behaviour. When workaholics achieve their goals, they are temporarily relieved. But if they fail, they fall into depression and/or inadequacy.

Consider the story of Sarah, a talented artist. Sarah loved painting, finding joy and fulfilment in the act of creating. However, she found herself increasingly motivated by external factors and became addicted to painting excessively - the praise of others, the potential for financial success, the pressure to create 'marketable' art, while painting for long hours daily. This inner drive for external validation began to drain her passion, leaving her feeling stressed and unfulfilled. It was only when she shifted back into intrinsic motivation, painting for the sheer love of it, that she was able to reconnect with her passion and find joy in her art again.

⇒ Key Two Renaissance Question ⇐

If you have been caught up in external factors, and lost sight of your inner drive, you can break this destructive behaviour habit by completely shifting your focus. The next time you start judging yourself from this lens, STOP! Instead, ask yourself:

> ➤ "Why am I doing this?"

Instead of obsessing about your outcomes, focus on your values. Be kind to yourself and remind yourself of your previous exercises. Trust the process, as you become a new Renaissance Person, shedding the old you, one step at a time.

As we reach the end of this chapter and approach the final segment of part one, take a moment to recognize the empowerment derived from the newly gained insights and self-discovery. Each turned page has propelled you closer to unravelling the intricate layers of your authentic self. Continue to write your thoughts and answers in your notebook, to help you create your personal rebirth and don't forget to celebrate yourself, as each step is a win.

⇒ Key Two Final Thoughts ⇐

- How have you recently applied your talents since reading this chapter?

- Which talent/gift provided you with the greatest sense of joy and contentment?

- What fresh insights have you gained about yourself?

- Have you been practicing any of the detachment techniques?

- How are you feeling at this moment?

- Have you been consistent with the all the NLP exercises we have shared so far?

- How do you feel after applying the NLP exercises?

- What was your latest victory, and how did you celebrate?

Remember like any tool, the more you use it, the easier it is to use.

PART II

PIVOTAL INTERACTIONS

PART II
PIVOTAL INTERACTIONS

Key Three | Deciphering Acts of Love as the Compass for Bold Actions

Take massive action. There is no other way.

Anthony Robbins

Deciphering is the ability to discern well, to perceive the subtle differences between things. In the context of values, discernment allows us to distinguish between actions motivated by love and those motivated by duty. While duty is important, actions motivated by love are often more fulfilling and aligned with our true values.

For instance, consider the story of Mark, a dedicated doctor. Mark was driven by a sense of duty, working long hours, and sacrificing his personal life for his career. However, he found himself feeling burnt out and unfulfilled. This reduced his performance at work and gave him trouble concentrating. One day his poor decision making, and lack of concentration nearly ruined his life. He prescribed the wrong medication to a patient. Thankfully the pharmacist spotted the mistake, before filling the subscription and had a private word with the doctor. Mark had to take a step back and evaluate where and why he had got to the point of working out of duty.

It was the wake-up call that he needed, and it was only then, that he began to discern between the two that he was able to find the balance he needed. He realized that while he loved helping others, he also needed to take care of himself by working less hours. He began to set boundaries, prioritizing his well-being alongside his work. This allowed him to continue serving his patients efficiently, while also living in alignment with his values.

You don't need a major epiphany like Mark's to find out if you're acting from love or duty. You can take the time to reflect on your current daily routine and ask yourself:

> ➤ "Why am I doing this, because I want to or because I feel like I should be?" also ask yourself;
>
> ➤ "When I finish this task, do I feel happy, energized, a huge sense of accomplishment? Or negative feelings?"

Make a note of your feelings in your special notebook. Clearly if you feel energized and truly value what you're doing, then you're driven by love. However, if you're engaging in an activity due to a sense of duty, feel emotionally disconnected during the process, or end up feeling depleted afterward, what does this indicate to you?

Always try to take time to be still and listen to your inner voices, instead of the outside voices of the world, that try and pull you in multiple directions. This is the practice of discernment; this is how you truly judge between actions of love or duty.

Learning to listen to your heart also helps you to discern what is truly right for you, you can start practicing discernment right now by taking a deep breath and asking yourself "What am I feeling right now?" Your daily peer pressure, doubt and external demands will have no choice but to halt and be still will you discern your authentic self. You may experience a sense of fear of inadequacy or even fear of rejection. These are the other chronic fears that can paralyze people, it's the ego's defence system locking in place to try and keep you trapped.

Facing your fears empowers you to align with your values and underscores the importance of legitimate fear as a valuable guide. Our genuine fears serve as crucial cautionary signals that steer us toward wisdom. Though they may initially appear unwelcome, these fears operate as our guardians, pointing us in the right direction. That's why it's essential to cultivate your discernment. When we heed our legitimate fears, we identify potential risks and challenges, enabling us to make informed choices. Essentially, our fears function as compasses, directing us towards both safety and personal growth, as they reveal our deepest desires hidden beneath. These fears drive us to confront our limitations and explore our true capabilities, demonstrating that within each fear lies an opportunity for triumph and thriving. They also motivate us to be consistently guided by love. By acknowledging and respecting our fears and utilizing discernment, we learn to navigate life's unpredictable terrain, ultimately emerging stronger, wiser, and better prepared for whatever challenges lie ahead, all while remaining true to our values. This journey leads us to freedom, breaking down the greatest barrier between you and your calling, and dispelling fear as the main obstacle of hope.

Discernment means to look at your deeper feelings and being truthful about where these deeper feelings will lead to. Are your feelings pleasant and lead you to feel empowered, positive and/or happy, or do they take you to a place of shame, regret, emptiness or just an overall bleak situation? These are the warning signs to help you realise if you are on the right path, or need to take immediate action to reroute so that you do not have a serious wakeup call like Mark. Using your discernment, by taking the time to contemplate your emotions can guide you away from surface-level benefits, misguided obligations, or sheer despair, enabling you to uncover your authentic path in life.

When we fully embrace and embody our core values, it brings about powerful emotions, enhancing our overall happiness and energy levels. Living authentically in accordance with our deepest values allows us to be our true selves, fostering a sense of fulfilment and contributing to a more meaningful life. This alignment with our values serves as a source of genuine happiness and vitality, emphasizing the significance of self-awareness in cultivating a well-balanced and contented existence. Approach the practice of deciphering your values with kindness towards yourself, embracing the wisdom it imparts. Make use of being introspective so you can transition from obscurity to heightened enlightenment.

When you follow your heart, you will be able to discern the difference between your true direction in life and not the compass that your friends and family may try to steer you in. We are all here to grow, expand, create. Psychologists note that our decision-making is often influenced by our visions of the future. Within these visions of our future self, we conceptualize both our best and worst potentials, drawing inspiration from those around us to shape these possibilities. While there might not be a direct quote on this specific topic, Carl Jung, a renowned psychologist, often touched upon the concept of this, which involves discovering and integrating one's true self. He once said, "Your vision will become clear only when you look into your heart. Who looks outside, dreams; who looks inside, awakes."[7] This sentiment encourages individuals to explore their inner selves, your inner compass, including your unique gifts, guiding you in the direction to a more authentic and fulfilling life.

Sometimes we base our potential selves through people we know. You can see this in the example of Mahatma Gandhi. Gandhi initially pursued a legal career, studying law in London, at the insistence of his mother. Upon attaining his legal qualifications, he relocated to South Africa, prompted by economic challenges hindering his career prospects when he went back to his home country. While he lived in South Africa he experienced racial discrimination, sparking a sense of injustice and a search for a greater purpose. Gandhi's transformation began when he encountered the philosophy of nonviolent resistance. Influenced by his readings, particularly of Henry David Thoreau, and inspired by the teachings of Jesus Christ, he developed a new vision for his life. Ultimately torn between the legal profession and a higher calling for justice and social change, Gandhi embarked on a path of civil disobedience and nonviolent protest. His commitment to both the law and a greater cause, much like Sir Thomas More, led him to success in both realms. Gandhi played a crucial role in India's struggle for independence and became an iconic figure in the global fight for civil rights and justice. His ability to navigate two seemingly divergent paths showcases the complexity of individual journeys and the fusion of different aspirations into a singular impactful legacy.

⇒ Key Three Exercise Describe & Visualize Your Ideal Self ⇐

Now it's time to determine the best possible version of you. There has been a lot of research by psychologists, showing that when you write about the best version of yourself, you're able to gain better clarity, well-being, and greater health.[8] For the next five days, spend ten to twenty minutes, somewhere quiet and alone, along with your notebook and do the following:

Close your eyes, take a few slow, deep breathes, and then see yourself as you would be if all your dreams and desires came true. What does it look and feel like? Write everything that you visualized down in as much detail as possible in your notebook and then pack your notebook away.

Over the next few days, repeat the process in the same way. On the final day, read over your four lists and combine all of them, writing a final detailed description of your ideal self.

Review what you have written by asking yourself how you feel about this 'ideal self' that you see. Are you content? Jovial? Thrilled?

If positive emotions are not evoked when thinking of your ideal self, ask if this is your best possible self or someone else's. If it is not really your true desires and represent who you are, re-do the exercise again, this time writing about your own deepest desires.

To help you gain clarity on values & eliminate your fears, take another look at your description of your ideal self, and discover more about your direction by asking yourself the following:

1. Are there any items on your previous list that seem like a dream deferred?

2. Is there anything on the list, or not listed that you have been wanting to do for some time and have not completed it yet?

3. Do you feel an inner longing to move in a certain direction?

If you come up against the feeling of fear while answering any of the above questions, you can ask yourself:

➢ "What am I really afraid of?"
➢ "What is the worst thing that can happen?"
➢ "Is this realistic and if so, how?"

Manifesting your future with hopeful thinking

Now that you know your ideal self, the next step in the right direction is to breath some life into your visualization. A continuous interplay exists between your current reality and the aspirations you hold. Many individuals feel disheartened by the gap between their ideals and their actual circumstances, resorting to aimless distractions. This segment introduces robust strategies rooted in psychology and NLP to narrow this divide, aiding you in setting, sustaining motivation, and plotting paths toward your goals.

Healthy individuals are in a perpetual state of evolution, pursuing objectives that are significant, quantifiable, and manageable. Through the guidance of your internal compass and the exercises in this book, you've unearthed a purposeful direction. Next you need to craft explicit, affirmative goals to steer your actions. So instead of expressing a vague wish, envision specific endeavours, and take tangible steps to realize them. I will use a personal specific goal of mine, I wanted to serve in my community, so I researched local non-profits, chose two of the charities that my values aligned with (rehabilitation of DV victims and youth independent living). I wanted to help make a larger impact within both social impact 501(c)3's that I chose and knew that both of them were very influential within the community I lived in. I reached out both charitable institutions to find out the steps on how I could volunteer and then started to put my action behind my intentions by actively helping. Being specific with my once vague goal of supporting my community, really helped me with taking positive action consistently, until it became a habit.

Research indicates that specific, positive goals not only amplify psychological well-being but also boost effectiveness. Set ambitious goals that challenge without overwhelming, fragmenting grand aspirations into achievable sub-goals. Emphasize the process rather than fixating on outcomes. Cement your commitment to your goal by jotting it down somewhere that you will see regularly, you could use post-it notes or even your phone, these reinforce your resolve.

After defining your goal, cultivate your motivation. Make a habit of putting your post-it notes somewhere that you can see daily and if you're using your phone, set a reminder so you can review your desired results daily. Picturing yourself accomplishing the goal and embracing the excitement, wear a smile as you welcome this new reality into your life. Recall a past triumph, a challenge you conquered, and the skills you employed while achieving it. Envision using these skills in your current pursuit. Shed false humility, discard feelings of inadequacy, and refrain from self-deprecation. Instead, consider someone you admire—someone too engaged in the adventure of life to indulge in personal put-downs.

If you catch yourself belittling your abilities, pause, take a deep breath, and focus on the present. Be extra gentle to yourself, accepting yourself and where you're at, while embracing life's adventure. In this crucial time, sustain your energy and positive momentum by ensuring you get adequate sleep, while consuming wholesome food, and engaging in regular exercise. It will help keep you in the right frame of mind. Only surround yourself with positive individuals who encourage and celebrate your progress, no matter how small.

Tap into the boundless energy of gratitude, as Denis Prager once said, "Of all the characteristics needed for both a happy and morally decent life, none surpasses gratitude".

Addressing Challenges

While accomplishing your new endeavour, most of you will have so much zeal, but then abandon that passion when obstacles arise. Your solid plan in place is considered as your guide to lead you to your goal, which will also help you overcome the hindrances that will arise. Another way you could look at your plan is like your pathway to success. If you wanted a holiday abroad, you would plan accordingly. First you would look for flights, hotels, your journey to and from the airport etc., as you would want to be as prepared as possible. The way to unlock your Renaissance is to plan your journey of renewal, just as strategically as you would for a holiday abroad. Using these guides to navigate toward your main objective.

- When you look at your post-it notes, or your objective reminders that you saved on your phone, visualize yourself accomplishing your goals and ask yourself, "What do you need to get there?" Then write down all of the specific steps.

- If you need develop a skill, or find out additional information, learn the skill needed, do your research, and if needed seek out additional help. Asking for help is a smart move and is also a great way to enlarge your current network. Fostering mutually beneficial friendships with individuals who uplift your new journey will help you unlock your Renaissance much quicker, as there is strength in numbers.

- Prepare for potential obstacles and challenges by anticipating roadblocks. Develop backup plans, ensuring that you have viable alternatives in case your primary path is obstructed.

- If a situation doesn't go as planned, formulate lessons from the experience, explore an alternative solution, or adjust your objective if needed. The key is to continue progressing and not stay stagnant.

Kim used these skills to move from sadness to victory. She embarked on her journey of becoming a lawyer, like her late father. Up until now she had run a clothing store with her sisters, but over the course of a year had researched how to achieve her goal. She began by enrolling to obtain a bachelor's degree, however after a few months Kim knew that this was not the route for her. The classes were boring, and she wasn't retaining the information she read from her books. She was failing all of her quizzes, but she was aware that without her degree, she would not be able to take the Law school admission test (LSAT), which is needed to get into Law school. Kim kept persevering and reminding herself of her end goal.

With advice from her professor, she determined she would need a new pathway, joining a legal apprenticeship program, which allowed her to study the law and gain practical experience without attending traditional law school. This alternative path is often referred to as "reading the law" or participating in a legal apprenticeship. Six months into her legal apprenticeship program, her passion for criminal justice reform, and her journey to become a lawyer was evident, however she was not gaining the hands-on experience she wanted. Kim wanted to be more intentional with her hands on work experience, and work on mass media law protects. Every time she met someone new, including her new friends she had met on the course, Kim would ask if they knew a way she could increase her knowledge of law, with more elevated practical experiences. She heard so many no's, yet still continued to ask people. Eventually, a few months later, her friend Pete asked if she was still looking as he knew just the person, and introduced her to a celebrity attorney called Brittney, who he had met at an event. Brittany owned firm that specialised in criminal justice advocacy. She agreed to let Kim help work on various criminal justice cases and got her involved in efforts to secure clemency for individuals serving lengthy prison sentences. This helped Kim's efforts to contribute within her targeted industry during her apprenticeship. Today she's the proud owner of one of the top Law firms in California. Kim's hope skills helped her become an exceptional lawyer.

⇒ Key Three NLP Activity to Develop Hopefulness ⇐

If you're struggling with remaining hopeful, here is an NLP activity to improve your hopefulness by creating a positive anchor. Anchors in NLP are stimuli that trigger a specific emotional state. Here's a step-by-step activity for you to try:

➢ **Choose a Peaceful Environment:** Find a quiet and comfortable space where you won't be disturbed.

➢ **Recall a Hopeful Memory:** Close your eyes and think of a moment in your life when you felt incredibly hopeful. It could be an achievement, a joyful experience, or a time when you overcame adversity. Fully immerse yourself in the details of that memory.

➢ **Engage Your Senses:** As you recall the hopeful memory, engage your senses. What did you see, hear, feel, and perhaps even smell or taste in that moment? Pay attention to the sensory details that make the memory vivid.

➢ **Create a Physical Anchor:** Choose a simple physical gesture or touch that you can associate with this hopeful feeling. It could be placing your hand on your heart, touching your fingertips together, or any other gesture that feels natural to you.

➢ **Associate the Gesture with Hope:** Once you've chosen your physical anchor, reconnect with the hopeful memory and, at the peak of that positive emotion, perform the chosen gesture. Repeat this process several times to solidify the connection between the gesture and the feeling of hopefulness.

➢ **Test Your Anchor:** Now, whenever you want to evoke a sense of hopefulness, use the physical anchor you've created. Perform the gesture and allow the positive emotions associated with hope to flow through you.

Write down your results in your Renaissance journal. Remember, be gentle on yourself as you try this new method and repeat this activity regularly. Repeating this exercise over time helps to condition your mind to associate the physical anchor with a hopeful state, providing you with a valuable tool to access hopefulness whenever needed.

Using Your Inner Navigation

Now that you have unlocked the map to your desired destination, don't let your wins or the pull of daily life make you take a wrong turn. Remember to use your inner navigation to stay on track.

Napoleon, born in Corsica in 1769, became a military general during the French Revolution and rose through the ranks rapidly. His military brilliance and charismatic leadership allowed him to seize power in a coup d'état in 1799, establishing himself as the First Consul of France. Over the next decade, he transformed the French Republic into the French Empire and, in 1804, crowned himself Emperor.

Napoleon's early successes on the battlefield, including the victories at Austerlitz and Jena, solidified his reputation as a military genius. However, his thirst for more power and territorial expansion led to a series of disastrous campaigns. The invasion of Russia in 1812, marked by the harsh Russian winter and logistical challenges, resulted in the loss of the vast majority of Napoleon's army. Despite facing defeat and abdication in 1814, Napoleon managed to escape exile and return to power in France for a brief period known as the Hundred Days. He faced the decisive Battle of Waterloo in 1815, where his military genius suffered a final defeat, leading to his second abdication and exile to the remote island of Saint Helena.

Napoleon's story serves as a moral lesson about the dangers of unchecked ambition. His initial rise to prominence showcased his military brilliance and strategic acumen, but his downfall was fuelled by an insatiable desire for quick territorial conquest and dominion, ultimately leading to his demise and the end of the Napoleonic era.

Napoleon ended up saying "Victory belongs to the most persevering"[9]. It reflects his emphasis on maintaining determination, persistence, and resilience as crucial elements for achieving success in various endeavours. This quote aligns with Napoleon's earlier reputation for being a driven and tenacious leader throughout his military and political career, emphasizing the importance of staying true to one's course despite the allure, in his case, more power and ambition.

In your life's journey, success will always have some type of challenge. Always remember to check your inner navigation to stay on the right path, that is in alignment with your values. "For every action, there is an equal and opposite reaction," according to Sir Isaac Newton's Third Law of Motion. Therefore, remember the decisions you make today, will affect your future, so stay prepared for resistance and keep working on your discernment.

Never Lose Hope

When you come head-to-head with resistance during your Renaissance, never lose hope. Facing significant and intricate challenges, certain individuals find themselves paralyzed, incapable of taking action, succumbing to the gradual toxicity of scepticism.

Emma was a charismatic and talented tv host. Her natural charm and wit drew audiences in, making her a rising star in the industry. Encouraged by her early successes, Emma aspired to climb higher and become a renowned TV personality. However, as she navigated the complexities of the media landscape, Emma encountered relentless challenges. Battling against industry expectations, dealing with cutthroat competition, and facing the pressures of maintaining a certain image took a toll on her. Despite her undeniable talent, Emma found herself entangled in a web of obstacles that threatened to overshadow her once-shining career.

With each setback, Emma's enthusiasm dimmed. The sparkle in her eyes, once reflective of her passion for hosting, dulled under the weight of constant scrutiny. Overwhelmed by the mounting challenges, she succumbed to the grasp of depression and helplessness. In a moment of despair, Emma stepped away from her television career. The once-exciting world of lights and cameras transformed into a haunting reminder of her shattered aspirations. Emma surrendered to cynicism, convinced that the world of television was reserved for those who played by the rules and conformed to expectations. She neglected her gifts, lost in the shadows of learned helplessness.

Dwayne 'The Rock' Johnson never started off as a well-known actor, producer, and successful businessman. He faced significant challenges early in his life, including financial struggles and a failed football career. After being cut from the Canadian Football League, he found himself broke without a clear path forward.

However, Dwayne Johnson did not let setbacks define his future. Taking a step back and asking himself what else can I do, he leveraged his charisma and athleticism, and transitioned to professional wrestling, where he became a global icon. The Rock was born, building on his wrestling success, he then set himself a new challenge and ventured into acting, facing a lot of initial scepticism in Hollywood.

Dwayne's determination and work ethic propelled him to become one of the highest-paid actors in the world. To overcome challenges and achieve success like Dwayne Johnson, individuals can draw inspiration from his ability to adapt, stay focused on long-term goals, and work tirelessly toward their passions. The Rock's journey exemplifies resilience, versatility, and the transformative power of dedication in the face of adversity. He followed his inner navigation system and never lost hope.

When facing major challenges, don't be like Emma and give in to the hardships, letting the problems overwhelm you. She dwelled on what she couldn't do, instead take a step back like Dwayne, and ask yourself "What can I do?" Use your hope skills to take positive action, value resilience and seek support in times of resistance.

⇒ Key Three Planning for Resistance Exercise ⇐

1. Think of something you can do with your gifts and set a goal that you can achieve in the next 3-6 months. If you think it will take you longer than that, then break your goal into smaller sub-goals.

2. Write down realistic weekly goals that you can execute, that will lead you to your end goal.

3. Think of possible areas where you could face resistance, or challenges that could arise. Be resourceful and think outside of the box like Dwayne Johnson. Look at alternative pathways to unlock your success and ask yourself "What else can I do?" be as creative as you can. Don't be afraid to change your approach or even tweak your goal. If the resistance you foresee is fear or doubt coming from within, take a moment to meditate and redo the NLP exercise you completed in this chapter.

4. Last but not least, be extra gentle with yourself, you are unlearning to relearn, and it takes time. Remember the saying 'Rome wasn't built in a day'!

As practice, in your Renaissance journal write down a new mini goal that is meaningful and manageable, followed with three steps to help you execute.

⇒ Key Three Reminders ⇐

Your choices today, affect your future. As you unlock more keys, remember to:

✓ Keep your eyes on the prize, your end goal should always come first, while using your inner navigation to guide you.

✓ Keeping building your hope and perseverance, even when there is resistance.

✓ Always look at your challenges as a way to be more creative and be fluid in your approach.

✓ There is strength in asking for help, and seeking additional information, skills, or tweaking or goal.

✓ Sometimes you can reach the same destination, via multiple routes. If there is a roadblock, or delays, and you change to another path, it may take you longer, but you still reach your destination.

Congratulations! You're ready to move beyond this chapter, as you're armed with the wisdom needed, and a palpable sense of readiness that awaits you in part two of your Renaissance journey. The narrative may evolve, but the lessons learned will undoubtedly serve as crucial keys needed to unlock a more enriched and purposeful existence. You're now ready to enter pivotal interactions.

PART II

Key Four | The Power of Positive Talk

Be careful how you're talking to yourself, because you're listening.

Lisa M. Hayes

What if I told you that 96% of adults admit to talking to themselves

daily?[10] Would it also surprise you if I told you that your self-talk amounts

to every single thing we think, and say to ourselves, every day. We think

somewhere between 12000 and 60000 thoughts, per day, and on average

80% of those thoughts are negative, and 95% are the same repetitive

thoughts from the day before, and the day before that.[11] When our

predominant thoughts lean towards the negative, and we perpetuate this

cycle through repetition, it's no surprise that our struggle for happiness

intensifies. Frequently, we remain oblivious to our internal dialogue, often

not recognizing the pervasive negativity. Even when we do become aware, the entrenched negativity may deceive us into believing it's a normal state of mind. Our language and thoughts do influence our behaviour and experiences. By empowering our language, we can completely shift our mindset and align our actions with our values and goals.

Despite Sally's many accomplishments and outward success within the asset management industry, she couldn't escape the shadows of negativity that clouded her mind. Her self-talk had become a relentless stream of self-criticism and doubt, echoing through her thoughts, day in and day out. Unbeknownst to Sally, this negative narrative was casting a dark veil over her life, leaving her perpetually unfulfilled.

One day she had an outburst at work, and she felt really depressed about her reaction and how she was feeling daily, it was time for a change. Sally had heard about the transformative power of Neuro-Linguistic Programming and was referred to me to guide her through this journey of self-discovery.

In the cosy confines of the NLP session, Sally began to unravel the layers of her subconscious mind. As a master practitioner, who is skilled in the art of language and perception, I helped Sally recognize the patterns of negative self-talk that had held her captive for too long. Together, we explored the root causes of these thoughts and gently reframed them into positive affirmations.

As Sally embraced the power of positive self-talk, a profound shift occurred within her. The once omnipresent cloud of negativity began to dissipate, making way for rays of optimism and self-love. Sally had unlocked the joy of acknowledging her accomplishments, the strength in embracing challenges, and the beauty of cultivating a mindset that fostered growth.

The transformation wasn't just internal; it manifested in Sally's external world too. Her relationships flourished, her work became more enjoyable, and a newfound zest for life emerged. The contrast between her previous state of perpetual unhappiness and the radiant joy she now exuded was palpable to those around her.

Her Renaissance journey taught Sally a valuable lesson – the immense impact that self-talk has on our well-being. She realized that by changing the script of her inner dialogue, she could rewrite the story of her life. Sally's story is a testament to the transformative power of positive self-talk and the profound influence it can have on our overall happiness. When we notice our self-talk is becoming destructive, you can change the language you use to shape your experiences and reactions to the world around you. Below is an NLP exercise that works well to reframe negative self-talk into positive affirmations. This activity involves exploring the negative self-talk, reframing it, and then reinforcing the positive affirmation.

⇒ Key Four 'Triple Description' NLP Exercise ⇐

1. Identify Negative Self-Talk

Identify a specific situation where you often experience negative self-talk. It could be related to self-esteem, confidence, or a specific aspect of your life. Describe the negative self talk in detail. It's encouraged to be very specific about the words, tone, and imagery associated with these thoughts.

2. Reframe the Negative Self-Talk

Now you need to reframe the negative self-talk into a more positive and empowering statement. Try and consider alternative perspectives and use language that only reflects self-compassion and strength. Explore how the reframed statement feels and sounds. Ensure that it resonates with you and is truly aligned with your values.

3. Reinforce with Positive Affirmation

Once the reframing is complete, create a concise and powerful positive affirmation based on your new perspective. The affirmation should counteract the negative self-talk and implement a sense of confidence and positivity. Repeat the positive affirmation aloud, focusing on the words, the emotions it invokes, and the belief in your new perspective. Repeat your new affirmation until it is ingrained within you.

Additional Tips to Enhance Your Reframing

When working with clients I encourage visualization: Visualize the positive outcome associated with your new affirmation. It's always useful to repeat the process and explore other instances of negative self-talk in different areas of your life to generalize the skill.

This activity engages both linguistic and visual modalities, allowing you to actively reframe your internal dialogue. It empowers you to shift from negative patterns to positive affirmations, fostering a more optimistic mindset over time. Remember to create a supportive and non-judgmental space throughout the process, so be gentle on yourself.

Improve Your Speech, Improve Your Health

It's not just self-talk that is detrimental to unlocking your Renaissance, but your ability be a master communicator with others is key. Your ability to master effective communication skills is key to a healthier and longer life. Yes, you read that right! According to ground-breaking research, completed by Dr. Janice Kiecolt-Glaser and Dr. Ronald Glaser, people who argue a lot, have weaker immune systems. Naturally, the poorer their immune system, the worse their health. They also completed a study with people who had life threatening diseases, the facilitators taught half of the group specific communication skills.

After meeting only six times and then coming together after five years, the subjects who had learnt how to express themselves effectively had a higher survival rate. Only 9 percent succumbed to their illness, unlike the group who were untrained, survival rate was almost 30 percent.[12] Consider the consequences of this study: even a slight enhancement in the ability to communicate and engage efficiently with others resulted in a significant 66 percent reduction in the mortality rate.

Honestly, with the numerous studies that have been verified to show that pessimistic communication is very damaging to your health, most people still don't believe it, even though there is a lot of evidence to prove it. In every case when we fail at conversations, we never feel better, mentally, or physically. When we are in stressful situations, differing

79

opinions, and intensified emotions, everyday discussions evolve into pivotal conversations. Paradoxically, the more critical the conversation, the greater the likelihood of mishandling it. Failing to navigate important conversations can have profound consequences, influencing diverse aspects of our lives, ranging from our professional pursuits and relationships to our overall personal well-being. In this chapter we're going to reinforce the key to positive conversations that will help you with your Renaissance.

The Approach to Engaging in Dialogue

How do you communicate effectively, especially in times of differing opinions and sometimes strong emotions? Given the fact that every person has their own experiences, habits, and comprehends situations differently, it doesn't sound like an easy task. In an earlier chapter, we previously discussed the importance of following your heart, and now we're embarking on a journey that once again centers around our hearts (are you starting to see a theme?). If you struggle to align yourself internally, navigating meaningful dialogue becomes challenging. In certain conversations, you may default to familiar communication patterns from your upbringing, such as engaging in debates, resorting to silence, or employing manipulation.

Karen found herself dialling the customer service number for her credit card. She had noticed an unauthorized charge and wanted to report it promptly. Karen aimed to quickly conclude the call and prepare for her up and coming zoom meeting, which was rapidly approaching. As the call connected to the bank, a robotic voice greeted her, followed by hold music that seemed to linger longer than necessary. Finally, a customer service representative named Dale picked up. "Hello, thank you for calling. My name is Dale. How can I assist you today?" he recited robotically.

Karen, determined to resolve the issue, explained, "Hi, Dale. I've noticed an unauthorized charge on my credit card, and I'd like to report it and get it sorted out, as soon as possible please."

Dale, seemingly distracted with voices in the background, at the call centre he worked at, responded, "I'm sorry, could you repeat that? I didn't catch what you said."

Frustrated but determined, Karen repeated herself, "There's an unauthorized charge on my credit card, and I need to report it."

Dale, with a hint of impatience, replied, "I'm sorry, ma'am. Your voice is breaking up. I can't hear you clearly."

Karen sighed, already feeling exasperated, she screamed "Alright, let me try again. There is a charge on my credit card that I didn't make, and I need your help to resolve it."

Dale replied, "you do not need to yell at me ma'am!" He then reviewed Karen's account, they engaged in a series of back-and-forth, with Dale occasionally putting Karen on hold. The process was taking a long time, and both of them couldn't help but express their frustrations. Karen thought, 'why can't he just listen properly, and do what I need him to do?' Eventually Karen realised she was irate and getting a headache from her raised temper. She looked at her watch and realised she needed to be on her zoom meeting, any minute now. She took a deep breath and decided she needed to deescalate the situation. Karen lowered her tone, apologised for her attitude and Dale swiftly followed suit. He was able to resolve her issue, and Karen seemed to feel a sense of relief as the solution was in motion.

The problem within this story is not that their behaviour deteriorated, it was because the reasoning Karen had for calling, had completely disappeared. Not only had she forgot her motive for calling, but she also ended up with an unnecessary headache.

So how do we get the results we truly desire when having tense conversations? The first step is to look within. Most of the time, we're always looking outward, and pointing the finger. We say to ourselves, "Why can't this person just do xyz?" This delays us from engaging in actions that could facilitate dialogue and advancement. It's unsurprising that individual's adept at communication often reverse this reasoning, as they know that change starts within.

How Dare You

While it is accurate that there are instances when we are mere spectators in life's continuous series of confrontations, seldom are we entirely blameless. In most cases, we play a role in exacerbating the issues we encounter. Those who master their dialogue grasp this fundamental truth and embody the fundamental truth that "what and how, can I do better" They acknowledge that personal improvement always benefits them, and they also recognize that they are the only individuals they can actively change. Attempting to compel change in others often proves futile and counterproductive. Genuine change is a voluntary journey, a path one chooses to embark upon. It's a realization that dawns when someone recognizes the need for personal growth or transformation. In creating a supportive environment and embodying positive change within us, we create a space where others may be inspired to follow our suit. However, the desire for change must originate from within, driven by an individual's own willingness and readiness to unlock their transformative journey.

A peculiar irony resides in this observation. Those who understand the importance of beginning with self-improvement genuinely undertake that journey. As they focus on their personal growth, they naturally hone their communication skills to a high degree. That's when the irony unfolds – it is the most adept individuals, not the least skilled, who consistently strive to enhance their communication mastery.

Always one to question, "How can I do better?" and a notable example from the Renaissance, is Queen Elizabeth I of England, known for leading from the heart, effective leadership, and strong communication skills. Elizabeth I, who reigned from 1558 to 1603, is remembered as one of the most influential and successful monarchs in English history. Despite the challenges faced by women in the 16th century, she received an extensive education, including studies in languages, literature, history, and the sciences.

Elizabeth maintained a vibrant correspondence with leading scholars of her time, including Sir Francis Bacon. These letters revealed her intellectual curiosity, as she sought to stay informed about the advancements in various fields. Engaging with intellectuals allowed her to stay on top of the

Renaissance's intellectual currents and incorporate progressive ideas into her governance.

Her correspondence with scholars, and support for the arts showcased her dedication to self-development. Queen Elizabeth I was also a skilled orator and communicator. She delivered powerful speeches, addressing both her subjects and foreign dignitaries. One of her most famous speeches is the "Golden Speech," delivered to Parliament in 1601, where she expressed her dedication to her people and the state. Her eloquence and ability to master her communication skills helped her connect with her audiences which contributed to her reputation as a charismatic leader.

Nothing Stays Hidden

When it comes to having great dialogue, you always need to be ready to speak your truth, even if your voice shakes. There are times when we make irrational decisions, that we usually end up regretting. Sometimes we think that we can lie our way out of them, however nothing is more far from the truth. Have you heard of the saying, 'Nothing done in the dark, stays in the dark'? This is nothing short of the truth. What do we do, when we are in a compromising situation, where something we tried to hide is unmasked? How do we get back in alignment?

Navigating challenges demands a strategic approach, and in those moments, there's an undeniable power in embracing our truth. Honesty stands as the beacon of wisdom, guiding us through the aftermath of mistakes. While the misstep may already be in the rear-view mirror, unveiling the truth becomes a salvage operation for our integrity. In doing so, we not only demonstrate accountability but also etch a lasting impression on those witnessing the situation. After all, in the intricate dance of life, honesty remains the most profound and enduring policy. This is where critical conversations come into play, if used correctly, it will be the best damage control.

It was the late 1990's and Bill Clinton was seen as a popular and effective president. He had enjoyed high approval ratings during his first term in office, and his administration was marked by economic prosperity and a budget surplus. Clinton was often praised for his ability to connect with the public, and his policy achievements, such as welfare reform and balanced budgets, contributed to his positive image.

But then a scandal rocked the world when President Bill Clinton was entangled in a controversial affair with White House intern Monica Lewinsky. The news broke, creating a media frenzy and casting a shadow over Clinton's presidency. During a press conference on January 26, 1998, President Clinton faced the media to address the allegations. In that moment, his speech had just turned critical. Will he be honest and dispel the rumours, or choose the opposite option?

We call this a critical conversation because how Bill Clinton acts during his speech will not only set people's attitudes toward the President but will also have a huge impact on how other world leaders think about him. Does he walk the talk of honesty? Or is he a hypocrite, like many of the previous presidents and world leaders who came before him?

He decided to use the last 30 seconds of his six minutes and forty-five second speech to address the salacious rumours. Those thirty seconds went like this; "I did not have sexual relations with that woman, Miss Lewinsky. I never told anyone to lie, not a single time. Never. These allegations are false. And I need to go back to work for the American people."

As we watch Bill, something quite subtle happens, his jaw tightens and he leans forward, squinting, he lifts his right hand, and starts pointing to the crowd while talking. His motive has clearly changed from making the right choice to something less noble. When under attack and faced with pressure and strong opinions, we often make unwise decisions, and say things we don't mean.

As the scandal unfolded, it became clear that Clinton's initial denial was not accurate. Subsequent investigations revealed the truth, he had lied, not only to himself, but to the nation, and the world.

The scandal not only had political ramifications but also left an indelible mark on public perception and the legacy of the Clinton presidency, which could have been avoided, if he had led from his heart and spoke his truth. The events surrounding the affair and subsequent denial are remembered as a significant chapter in American political history, highlighting the complexities of truth, and accountability.

Embracing Truth in Communication

In the intricate tapestry of human interactions, the thread of truth weaves a foundation of trust, transparency, and authenticity. It is in acknowledging the importance of speaking the truth, even when it carries a negative connotation, that we unlock the transformative power of genuine communication.

At the heart of meaningful connections lies trust, a delicate element easily shattered by deceit. Choosing honesty, especially when confronted with challenges or uncomfortable realities, becomes the bedrock upon which trust is built. Whether in personal relationships, professional collaborations, or societal bonds, the authenticity of truth fosters an environment where trust can flourish.

Negativity, in the form of criticism, disagreement, or unwelcome news, is an inevitable aspect of the human experience. By choosing to speak the truth, even when it casts a shadow, we pave the way for constructive conflict resolution. Transparency about challenges allows for collective problem-solving, fostering an atmosphere where growth and improvement can thrive.

When we express the truth, including the negative aspects of a situation, we reveal our authentic selves. Authenticity, in turn, forms the basis for genuine connections. People resonate with sincerity, and sharing the truth, even if it is uncomfortable, invites others to connect with us on a deeper level. It is through these authentic connections that relationships gain resilience and depth.

When navigating personal relationships, the healing power of truth cannot be overstated. While delivering negative truths may be uncomfortable in the short term, the long-term benefits include the restoration of trust, emotional well-being, and the potential for stronger connections.

In organizations, communities, and societies, the importance of truth-telling extends to the creation of a culture of integrity. Leaders who prioritize transparency, even when delivering unfavourable news, set the tone for an environment where ethical standards are upheld. Such cultures not only weather storms more effectively but also attract individuals who value honesty and authenticity.

In conclusion, speaking the truth, even when it carries negativity, is a courageous act that transcends momentary discomfort. It lays the groundwork for trust, authentic connections, and personal and collective growth. As we embrace the importance of truth in communication, we contribute to a world where honesty is valued, integrity is celebrated, and genuine connections form the fabric of our shared human experience.

Mastering The Art of Persuasive Communication

So far, we've dedicated considerable effort to readying ourselves for meaningful and effective conversations. Key takeaways include ensuring our intentions are genuine, staying attuned to crucial dialogues—particularly when individuals feel uneasy—and restoring a sense of safety when necessary. Having equipped ourselves to express opinions and viewpoints, the next challenge emerges. Often, we default to autopilot with casual greetings like "hey, how are you?" etc., yet depending on the conversation's nature, emotions may come to the forefront, especially if our words don't unfold as expected. Contrary to our desire for flawless interactions, certain discussions tend to bring out our less-than-optimal behaviour. To improve our capacity for offering difficult conversations, let's explore a real-life example that Eve had experienced. All of the crucial skills for expressing ideas that could potentially trigger defensiveness in others, were applied, leaving a favourable outcome. The goal is to communicate openly, ensuring that our thoughts are conveyed in a manner that fosters a safe environment for others to listen, respond, and engage effectively.

Eve, an assistant manager, found herself in the midst of a challenging project where collaboration between her colleagues was key, however everyone was not pulling their weight. What also made things extremely difficult was that the manager, called Jen, was also micromanaging her and some of the team members. No one had the confidence to tell Jen how they felt, and it was becoming increasingly difficult to work together, when they felt that some individuals were being treated differently. The staff comprised of diverse individuals with varying perspectives, needed to navigate through critical decisions. Aware of the potential for conflicting opinions, Eve decided to try and apply the five essential skills she had recently learned during our session. She wanted to articulate her thoughts effectively without triggering defensiveness.

I've decided to share the testimonial a little differently than in previous chapters, by dissecting each part of the conversation, with the skills Eve used, while also noting the response for her team members. I have then listed the skills individually underneath, in hopes that this will give you a more vivid depiction. Let us follow Eve while she uses her persuasive charm;

Eve: (Empathy & Safety in Action)

"As you're aware, we are still a little out on our timeline, for our huge project. Before we dive in, I want to acknowledge the different talents we all bring to the table. Each of us has a unique viewpoint shaped by our experiences. I want to take a moment to recognize and appreciate the diversity we have here. Is there anything anyone wants to add to my statement?"

Team Member 1: (Resulted in Active Engagement)

"I'm concerned about the timeline we have left. I think we might be biting off more than we can chew."

Eve: (Active Listening and Humility)

"I hear your concerns about the timeline. It's a valid point, and I want to ensure we explore it thoroughly. Can you share more about your specific worries and any suggestions you might have?"

Team Member 2: (Feedback with a Purpose)

"I think we should reconsider the approach. It feels a bit ambitious, and we might be overlooking potential pitfalls."

Eve: (Constructive Feedback with Confidence)

"I appreciate your input. I truly believe that there are elements of truth within what you just shared. I also feel that maybe if we all make a mental note of our strengths and weaknesses, we can chip in, and help someone else, if we finish our tasks early on that particular day. I also think we need to make sure we are not overstepping boundaries with others, while also making sure that we treat everyone the same. I include myself and hold myself accountable. If we are all doing our part, we will thrive better. Jen, I know as a manager you're under extreme pressure as well, but it would really help all of us, if you give us the space to utilize our skills and problem-solving capabilities. I have confidence in our team's ability to succeed, just as you do, otherwise you would not have hired us. It would help us increase our creativity and ownership of our work. We could collectively optimize our workflow for greater efficiency and productivity, which I think will foster a culture of trust and empowerment within the team, leading to even more positive outcomes. Now let's delve into the potential pitfalls you're foreseeing. Your insights are valuable, and together we can address any challenges head-on."

Team Member 3: (Crystal-Clear Communication)

"I think you make some strong points that I agree with, however I'm still a little unsure that I understand the overall strategy. Could you clarify the end goal and how we plan to achieve it, with the new insights you shared? Does it mean that we need to increase our workload, or do we carry on as we have been doing? I hope I am not asking to many questions, I just want additional assurance, that I fully understand."

Eve: (Promoting a Culture of Openness)

"Absolutely, transparency is key. Let me break down the strategy and address any uncertainties. I want everyone to feel comfortable expressing their thoughts. So far, we are all feeling the demands of our tasks, so I want to alleviate that for everyone involved. If there are questions or uncertainties, now is the time to voice them, and I will respond accordingly. Is that fair enough Jen? Let's start with your response and then go around the room, one by one."

Let's look at these skills individually:

91

> ➤ **Cultivating Empathy & Safety**

Eve began by understanding her colleagues. She knew that they all had different viewpoints, acknowledging their concerns, and appreciating their unique perspectives. This empathetic approach laid the groundwork for everyone to feel safe and allowed for open communication with condemnation.

> ➤ **Active Listening & Humility**

During team discussions, Eve actively listened to her colleagues, without any interruptions, ensuring that their voices were heard and validated. This not only made them feel valued but also created an atmosphere where everyone felt safe expressing their opinions. Eve had the humility to understand that everyone should have an input, as their views were just as valuable. She knew that she did not need to win her way, rather her viewpoint would be a starting point but not the final word. Her way of thinking could also be changed once she receives new information from other teammates. This means she is willing to express her way of thinking, while encouraging others to do the same.

> ➤ **Constructive Feedback with Confidence**

When Eve needed to share feedback or differing viewpoints, she framed her thoughts constructively. Instead of critiquing, she focused on the potential for improvement and growth, fostering a collaborative spirit among the team. Eve also used her skilled dialogue to confidently say what needed to be said, unlike some of her other team members, Eve knew that her opinion deserved to be heard by the people that needed to hear it. She knew that she could speak confidently, without attacking others or causing undue offense.

➢ Clarity and Transparency

Eve prioritized clear and transparent communication. She expressed her ideas with precision, avoiding ambiguity. This clarity helped prevent misunderstandings and provided a solid foundation for productive discussions. When one of the team members asked for more clarity, Eve was willing and able to do so.

➢ Encouraging Open Dialogue

Recognizing that open dialogue throughout the conversation was crucial for team success, Eve actively encouraged her colleagues to express their thoughts freely. By creating an environment where diverse opinions were welcomed, Eve promoted a culture of collaboration.

As a result of Eve's intentional application of these skills, the team not only successfully navigated through the intense dialogue, but they also powered through the project challenges, and strengthened their working relationships. The open and safe communication Eve displayed, led to an environment that allowed each team member, including the manager to contribute their concerns without fear of defensiveness, ultimately leading to a more innovative and effective outcome. Eve's commitment to enhancing her advocacy skills not only benefited the project but also left a lasting positive impact on her manager and the rest of the team dynamics. The team, once tense, now felt empowered to tackle the challenges ahead with a united front.

⇒ Key Four Delicate Reminders ⇐

Remember when the going gets tough and conversations are delicate:

- ✓ Stay focused on the goal you have set. What do you really want out of this conversation and how can dialogue help you get there?
- ✓ The only person you can control is yourself, so at the forefront of your mind, try to control how you react to the responses you receive from the other person/s. Do not become the victim.
- ✓ Your behaviour reveals your true motives,
- ✓ It's imperative to always be honest when you communicate, as the truth cannot be hidden or masked
- ✓ Speaking the truth, even when it carries negativity, is a courageous act that lays the groundwork for trust
- ✓ If you're about to have a difficult conversation with someone, start the conversation by sharing the least controversial, but most persuasive portions.
- ✓ Encourage the other people involved to share their facts and/or stories

✓ Make it a safe and open space for others to share any opposing or different viewpoints they may have.

You don't need to be perfect to make a start and repetition creates success. You have unlocked the key to positive communication and are ready to move onto the third and final stage of this book. You have come so far on your journey of Renaissance. The final chapters to follow, will reveal how to utilise everything you have learnt so far. In your Renaissance journal, write down how you celebrate yourself for making it this far.

PART III

LEVERAGING
RENAISSANCE PRACTICES
FOR YOUR BENEFIT

PART III
LEVERAGING RENAISSANCE PRACTICES FOR YOUR BENEFIT

Key Five | Having Faith in Your New World

Faith is taking the first step, even when you don't see the whole staircase.

Martin Luther King Jr

In the first two parts of this book, you began to discover your gifts, change your mindset, discern your true values, and mastered your communication skills to help you enter the fullness of your Renaissance journey. The next three chapters will take you into the final portion of this book. You will get the keys to unlock the guidance and support you need to embrace and sustain your newfound purpose, so you can live your Renaissance life to its fullest.

All of the Renaissance individuals' ideals and dreams found strength in consistent engagement with faith, self-reflection, contemplation, disciplined perseverance, artistic involvement, literature, physical activity, and also community. Initially, these rituals might appear disconnected from contemporary life. You may question, "How can activities like meditation, dinner and a movie with a friend, or creating art contribute to my life's purpose?" The efficacy of these practices, defying conventional reasoning, frequently escapes our grasp, concealed within the profound wisdom of the Renaissance. These invaluable tools transcend mere techniques.

The distinction between a technique and a practice is in their impact and nature. A technique is a method or skill applied to achieve a specific outcome, essentially doing something for you. On the other hand, a practice involves regular, intentional engagement in an activity that has a transformative effect on you, doing something to you. While a technique is a tool or method with a specific purpose, a practice goes beyond the immediate goal, contributing to personal growth, mindset, or well-being over time.

This concept aligns with the teachings and philosophies of various thought leaders. Many spiritual and personal development teachers emphasize the transformative power of consistent practices, (or habits), over just techniques. Notable figures such as Eckhart Tolle, and Deepak Chopra often discuss the profound impact of regular practices on one's inner growth and well-being. The proof of these practices can be seen throughout history, in all the Renaissance Men and Women, along with the greats of our modern day, and numerous people ranging in age from their teens to the age of retirement. It's the habits of all highly successful achievers.

Living Out One's Faith

The first of these practices is faith. Let's have a look at the word and its meaning in the dictionary; a complete trust or confidence in someone or something, or a strong belief in God or in the doctrines of a religion, based on spiritual apprehension rather than proof. You could also look at faith like embracing the inherent harmony of the cosmos and our interconnectedness with it. It empowers us to confront difficulties with resilience and uncover significance in our day-to-day existence. Amid the perpetual uncertainties and adversities of our contemporary era, faith reassures us that our endeavours carry purpose and that life, in its intricate unfolding, maintains a meaningful coherence.

No matter how you characterize your individual faith, embracing a sense of calling involves the conviction that your abilities and ventures can create a meaningful impact. Across various spiritual traditions throughout history, there has been a shared affirmation that we are integral to the expansive tapestry of life. In the bible one of the verses that confirms such a notion, it reads as follows;

'For I know the plans I have for you, declares the Lord, plans to prosper you and not to harm you, plans to give you hope and a future.'
Jeremiah 29:11

Despite variations in doctrines, individuals in the Renaissance commonly participated in regular religious services and engaged in daily prayer. Their faith served as a sustaining force during plagues, political upheavals, and even wars, providing assurance that their lives possessed inherent purpose.

⇒ Key Five Renaissance Questions ⇐

In our contemporary world, numerous individuals struggle with uncertainty, lacking an unseen foundation for support. Reflect upon whether you possess the faith necessary to uphold you in your life's purpose. Pause for a moment and introspect. Ask yourself the following;

> ➤ Do I feel that my life has purpose?
> ➤ Do I feel anchored in my world?
> ➤ Do I have a source of inspiration?
> ➤ Do I have the right support?
> ➤ Do I believe in the greatness within me?
> ➤ Am I ready to unleash my fullest potential to the world?

This chapter is designed to guide you in responding to these questions.

Deepening Your Faith

I have several friends who hold a profound sense of faith. Some of them are Christians, ranging different levels of faith, and my dearest friend in London is a devout Muslim. Others are Spiritual, sustained by their contemplative practice. Some friends are very active in their churches, mosques, and synagogues, while some of my friends find their inspiration in the red dessert of Sedona, Arizona.

Whatever your personal faith, it is deepened by regular practice. Whether through meditation, introspection, or formal ceremonies, engaging consistently in the observances of your faith provides spiritual anchors to assist you in navigating life's journey. This chapter provides instances of faith practices, including expressions of gratitude, spiritual role modelling, and compassion. Certain practices may resonate with you more than others, but either way, please try them all, and choose at least one to repeat and make a regular habit.

Five Things You're Grateful For

The word "grateful" has its roots in the Latin word "gratus," meaning pleasing or thankful. Before, and during the Renaissance, people have paused to give thanks for their daily blessings. This ranges from Christian, Jewish, Muslim, Hindu and even Buddhist traditions. There is research that shows "counting your blessings" not only decreases your stress but also increases energy, alertness, a strong sense of meaning, great well-being, and overall positivity.[13]

Michelangelo Buonarroti, from the Renaissance period, renowned for his masterpieces like the Sistine Chapel ceiling, faced numerous challenges, including political turmoil and personal struggles. Despite these adversities, his deep faith and gratitude for his artistic talents became sources of inspiration. Michelangelo viewed his artistic abilities as gifts from a divine source, and this perspective fuelled his perseverance and

103

creativity. His unwavering faith and gratitude contributed to his ability to overcome obstacles and leave an indelible mark on the art world.

He would express his gratitude through his letters and poetry, which also provided insights into his spiritual and philosophical views. In his writings, Michelangelo had a deep appreciation for his creative abilities, and often expressed a sense of divine inspiration and gratitude for the artistic talents he believed were bestowed upon him by a higher power. For instance, in one of his sonnets, he acknowledged his artistic gifts as a divine blessing, from a transcendent source.

⇒ Gratefulness Exercise ⇐

For the next seven days, at the end of each day I want you to list at least 5 things you're grateful for. If you can also share your list with someone else and encourage them to share their list of 5 too.

When you get to the end of the week, have some time of reflection, and ask yourself if this exercise has made you feel more positive. List all the emotions it has made you feel. Some individuals experience an overall improvement in well-being, while others discover themselves noticing blessings and fresh opportunities throughout the week. Hopefully you will experience both and deepen your faith like Michelangelo Buonarroti.

Discovering Your Spiritual Mentor

For centuries, stretching beyond the Renaissance, individuals have reaped the rewards of having an influential spiritual role model—someone whose impact resonates through their lives. Numerous psychologists affirm that a positive role model can evoke feelings of elevation, joy, and inspiration, especially when witnessing or reading about acts of kindness. The Renaissance era, rich in culture, offered a plethora of spiritual mentors, we see through literature, St. Teresa of Avila chose St. Jerome, and St. Clare as her role models. Queen Elizabeth, I engaged in vibrant correspondence with leading scholars, such as Sir Francis Bacon. While finding spiritual mentors today maybe slightly more challenging, the pursuit to find one is invaluable. Have you encountered inspiration from someone close, a historical figure, or even via social media? Personally, I've discovered spiritual mentors through various channels — social media, books. I've even had the privilege of direct mentoring interactions, from Dr. Mike Murdock and Tony Robbins to reading about historical figures like Maria Woodworth-Etta, these mentors have played a pivotal role in shaping my faith and character, an idea supported by research in the field.

⇒ Find Your Spiritual Role Model Exercise ⇐

Take some time to contemplate, and in your Renaissance, journal write the answers down to the following questions, which will guide you to your spiritual role model.

> ➤ Think of a few people that you hold in high regard.
> ➤ What are their top three qualities?
> ➤ Be honest with yourself and write down if you already emulate these qualities, and if you don't what steps would you need to take to develop them?

> ➢ Take action and apply these qualities during the next week.

Some of the action steps you can take to get to know your spiritual mentor on a deeper level, is find out if they have an autobiography, if so, read it. You can also utilize the internet and do deep research, and/or if they are a role model that is still alive, check to see if they have live events in a city near yours. Make the investment and attend, I am sure you won't regret it.

Be Gentle with Yourself

During the Renaissance, some individuals grappled with an intense lack of self-worth, becoming consumed by their perceived flaws to the point of believing that not even the infinite grace of God could redeem them, leading to profound despair. Cultivating self-compassion serves as a safeguard against such hopelessness. Self-acceptance involves confronting our shortcomings with gentleness and understanding. While it's natural to feel disappointed when mistakes occur, it's crucial not to condemn ourselves. Psychologists recognize that giving ourselves grace is vital for emotional and spiritual well-being, effectively reducing stress and anxiety, amongst other negative emotions. Remember, acknowledge mistakes as part of your human experience and focus on what you can do differently moving forward, as everything is a learning experience.

⇒ **Key Five Self-Compassion NLP Exercise** ⇐

- **Setting the Scene**

Find a quiet and comfortable space where you won't be disturbed. Take a few deep breaths to centre yourself.

- **Positive Anchoring**

Close your eyes and recall a moment when you felt deeply loved, accepted, and at peace. It could be a memory with friends, family, or a serene place. As you vividly relive this moment, immerse yourself in the positive emotions associated with it.

- **Create a Positive Self-Image**

Visualize yourself in the mirror, radiating confidence, kindness, and self-love. Imagine the best version of yourself, free from self-criticism and full of self-compassion.

- **Powerful Affirmations**

Repeat positive affirmations aloud or in your mind. Choose phrases that resonate with you, such as:

"I am worthy of unlimited love and kindness."

"I embrace my imperfections with compassion."

"I am deserving of self-care and understanding."

- **Transform Negative Thoughts**

Identify a recurring negative thought or self-critical belief. Now, reframe it into a positive and compassionate statement. For instance, if you often think, "I'm not good enough," transform it into, "I am constantly growing and learning, and I am enough just as I am."

- **Anchoring the Positive Emotions**

Touch your thumb and forefinger together (creating an anchor) while fully immersed in the positive feelings and affirmations. Hold this anchor for a few moments.

- **Recall and Apply**

Whenever you encounter a challenging situation or negative self-talk, use your anchor. Gently touch your thumb and forefinger and recall the positive emotions, affirmations, and the transformed self-image. Allow these positive feelings to replace self-critical thoughts.

Repeat this exercise regularly to reinforce positive neural pathways and strengthen your self-compassion anchor. Remember, NLP exercises are most effective when practiced consistently. Adjust the affirmations of this exercise to fit your preferences and ensure it aligns with your personal journey toward self-compassion. This exercise will also help you become more mindful, staying in the present moment.

Practicing mindfulness, offers numerous benefits, including improved mental health, enhanced decision-making, increased productivity, and more meaningful relationships. Embracing the present, while being gentle with yourself, fosters gratitude, self-awareness, and a profound mind-body connection, contributing to an overall higher quality of life.

Persisting with Your Dreams

You're now halfway through 'having faith in your new world', and as you continue to move forward on your personal Renaissance, regular check-ins are vital for your optimal success. Without frequent evaluations, you might easily steer off track, swayed by different directions.

While studying at NYU, a friend of mine, called Jodie, failed to do check-ins while studying. Enchanted by the late nights and vibrant lights of Manhattan, she succumbed to the allure of fun, which ultimately led to her failing out of her program in the final year.

Remaining connected to your goals and values doesn't just keep you on track; it can also awaken your intuition, enabling you to identify opportunities and craft the life you've always envisioned. Breathwork coach Curtis, a single father, resided and worked in a very busy spiritual centre, located on Abbott Kinney, close to Venice Beach. Now that the restrictions from covid-19 had been lifted, he was constantly doing workshops at the spiritual hub. He started to feel tired, burnt out, and also feeling restless and discontent with residing in a state that was trying to force everyone to have a new vaccine, that had not been tested thoroughly enough.

Curtis began taking some time to reflect on where he was at in life, and as a result decided to have a conversation about how he felt with his daughter. They realized that they would prefer to live in a more rural area, in a state that has more than one season, so they began to look for pathways. He knew that he could essentially work from anywhere, as recently he had started doing some sessions online and his daughter was about to finish her last year in middle school. They decided to use the summer holidays to have a road trip. They would hire a convertible and drive up to Utah, hike at the Zion national park, then drive to Wyoming before returning to Los Angeles.

While in Utah, they felt a sense of freedom, and enjoyed the local attractions while relaxing. A week into their trip, they finally decided to finally visit the national park, named after the heavenly city, and they noticed a hawk that kept flying in circles just ahead of their car. Curtis felt intuitively to follow the hawk and got led to a gated community. The Hawk landed on the sign that had the office number, and Curtis's daughter told her dad it was a sign to call. They got through and asked for a viewing, parked the car up and looked at two units. The second unit was incredible, spacious, freshly painted, with a great view and let's not forget the well-kept garden. Curtis filled in the paperwork for the apartment that was twice the size of their current unit, but two thirds of the price, their first step in their journey to a new life.

Following their pathways, Curtis continued his online breathwork sessions, connected with a spiritual hub near Zion and moved his daughter to a great high school in Utah. His daughter really loved the new apartment, and Curtis decided to buy a dog to make their family complete. Nine months later, Curtis took another step, leaving his position at the spiritual hub, to be full time at his own establishment called breathwork cleanse. Today, as a mindfulness coach and breathwork training facilitator, he has more time on his hands and is living the life of his dreams.

By introducing you to the power of persisting with your dreams, and checking in with yourself, this second half of the chapter will help awaken the power of your intuition, giving you the will to keep following your heart and completely transform your life.

Looking Back to Look Forward

People in the Renaissance days would engage in Examen. This refers to a form of prayer or reflection associated with the spiritual exercises of St. Ignatius of Loyola. It involved a structured method of reviewing one's day, actions, and experiences to discern and deepen one's relationship with God. The Examen was often used as a reflective practice for spiritual growth and self-awareness. This practice involves short intervals of silence and solitude, a contemplative habit that stands in contrast to our busy, overscheduled culture. As you go on your daily tasks, stay focused on your direction, and what is truly essential for you.

Mastering the skill of directing our attention has a profound impact on our lives. By focusing your attention on your purpose, goals, and values, you transition from mere efficiency—juggling multiple activities in your day—to effectiveness, dedicating yourself to actions of genuine significance. Without moments of reflection, you risk being swayed by distractions, feeling overwhelmed, or being pulled in various directions without a clear understanding of the bigger picture. Your Examen becomes a time-saving practice, preventing you from investing time in things that lack true significance. Remember, consistent small actions yield monumental results. Establish a regular time and place for your Examen to introspect and align with your aspirations.

- ✓ Fifteen minutes in the morning as you plan your day
- ✓ Fifteen minutes at the end of the day, perhaps after dinner
- ✓ Five minutes before turning in for the night

Now that you have chosen a time for your Examen, the rest of this chapter will show you exactly how to complete it.

Modern Day Examens

From the Renaissance to today, an Examen generally includes the following four steps:

1. Focusing attention on your goals and values
2. A daily reflection to evaluate your actions based on these principles
3. Learn from your successes and failures
4. Plan to upgrade in the future

Daily Examens have become an important part of coaching and counselling. Many people today also include Examens into their lives. Amidst the high-paced world of a prestigious Michelin-starred restaurant, Paul, a talented chef, felt the strain of her demanding routine. Seeking solace, he turned to the Examen, and through this time of introspective, Paul identified the unnecessary complexities in his daily tasks. With newfound clarity, he streamlined his culinary efforts, focusing on dishes that aligned with his values and passion. The simple practice of the Examen became his guiding light, transforming Paul's culinary career into a source of deep fulfilment and purpose.

⇒ Key Five Examen Exercise ⇐

Now it's time for you to start your own Examen. You have already designated a moment to check in with yourself. Now, retrieve your Renaissance journal and record your responses to the following questions that are continued on the next page:

    a) Write down your direction/current goal

    b) Your guiding values

    c) What brought you great energy, happiness, peace, joy?

    d) What brought me confusion, depression, sadness, doubt, fear?

    e) What would I do differently next time, and why?

Consistently practicing the Examen daily is crucial. Contemplating your values, direction, and goals will help you stay connected with your dreams, while concentrating on consolations will provide inspiration. As you conclude your journey of having faith in your new world, take a moment to reflect on the questions we've delved into throughout this chapter.

⇒ Key Five Renaissance Questions ⇐

Now that you are at the end of having faith in your new world, pause for a moment, and contemplate on the following questions that we explored throughout the chapter. Write your answers in your Renaissance notebook;

➤ How did you feel after completing 'five things you're grateful for'? Did you experience more joy and opportunities?

➤ What did you learn when reading about spiritual mentors?

➤ Are you actively practicing being gentle with yourself?

➤ Which one of the three faith practices will be supporting you on the rest of your Renaissance journey?

➤ Are you using your Examen three times a day?

➤ Have you noticed a difference, and if so, what differences have you noticed?

➤ When you make a mistake, are you asking yourself 'what can I learn from this?

➤ How are you going to celebrate yourself for reaching the end of key five?

⇒ Key Five Reminders ⇐

When you embrace your life's purpose, the universe unfolds a realm of possibilities, comparable to having keys that unlock specific doors on your journey. You will welcome greater joy, peace and meaning to your life.

❖ It's crucial to continue to extend kindness to yourself

❖ Nurture your faith, with your faith practices

❖ Stay in the present moment at all times

❖ Stay the course, even when it becomes difficult

❖ Embrace the light of consolation with joy and gratitude

By incorporating the Examen into your daily routine, you empower yourself to live in alignment with your calling and utilize your gifts more effectively. This practice extends beyond personal benefits; as you channel your creative energies into your core values, you unlock fresh possibilities and discover innovative solutions to longstanding issues. In doing so, you contribute to alleviating disease, despair, and the perpetuation of violence, brightly illuminating the world with newfound sources of energy. As you cultivate a Renaissance within yourself, you become a person of hope, inspiring and renewing the patterns of our world.

PART III

Key Six | Finding Your Inner Serenity While Creating Your Life into a Masterpiece

Your life doesn't get better by chance; it gets better by change.

Jim Rohn

Renaissance philosophers recognized the vital interplay between action and contemplation in life. However, in our contemporary era, achieving this delicate balance has become challenging, thanks to the pervasive influence of technology, which has blurred the boundaries of our existence.

Tristan, a young man navigating the demands of freelance photography, the last year of high school and home, found himself overwhelmed by the incessant juggling act of life. During one of our NLP sessions, he realised how imbalanced his life had gradually unravelled, but through

117

introspection and guided reflection, Tristan came to a profound epiphany — the need for equilibrium and the pursuit of joy. We decided that he was going to implement strategies to balance his professional and personal spheres. Tristan's new goals was to meditate, delegate and reinforce his boundaries. As he left the session, the weight of adding these new goals overwhelmed him, as he wondered how he would be able to foster a harmonious blend in his busy life.

During the Renaissance, the lives of men and women followed a more serene pace compared to today's frenetic existence. Lacking modern technology, they adhered to natural cycles of action and contemplation. Daylight hours were dedicated to work, while evenings were spent immersed in reading by the gentle glow of candlelight. Their nights concluded early with a restful sleep, cultivating a lifestyle that embraced the harmony of daily rhythms. St. Teresa of Avila, St. John of the Cross, and philosophers like Michel de Montaigne, valued introspection, and contemplation by taking moments of meditation, prayer and even engaging in periods of silence. They credit such actions to helping them with live in their life's purpose, giving them the perseverance and persistence in times of need.

A portion of this chapter is the key to unlock reflective practices within your own Renaissance journey, and will help you balance your life with peace, clarity, and more wisdom.

The Practice of Reflection

Reflection, otherwise known as contemplation, is widely seen in many faiths, including Christianity, Judaism, Islam, Buddhism, and many more. There is research that shows that all forms of contemplation will laser focus your attention, which in turn will produce superior spiritual, mental, and physical health. You could describe contemplation, or reflection as meditation, during which you frequently experience profound feelings of tranquillity, clarity, and relaxation. The consistent practice of meditation can quietly reshape your life, fostering increased serenity, patience, clarity, and understanding.

There are numerous forms of meditation, but here are three widely practiced ones:

Mindfulness Meditation: Focuses on being present in the moment, observing thoughts and sensations without judgment.

Transcendental Meditation (TM): Involves silently repeating a mantra to achieve a state of relaxed awareness.

Loving-Kindness Meditation (Metta): Concentrates on cultivating feelings of compassion and love, often through repeating phrases or affirmations.[14]

Years of scientific inquiry have revealed the health benefits of the meditation practices I listed. It is known to boost the immune system and alleviates conditions such as stress-related anxiety, insomnia, panic disorders, PMS, skin disorders, high cholesterol, asthma, cardiovascular disease, chronic pain, depression, eating disorders, headaches, hypertension, substance abuse, and even stuttering. Meditation also has a positive impact on the brain by increasing activity in the left frontal lobe, which is associated with positive emotions. It fosters self-compassion, reducing anxiety and promoting mindfulness. By mitigating stress, which is linked to aging, meditation may contribute to maintaining a youthful state. Studies also indicate that meditation is associated with enhanced self-actualization and self-awareness, increased empathy, maturity, emotional intelligence, and improved memory.[15, 16, 17, 18]

⇒ Key Six Contemplative Practice Exercise ⇐

You can start practicing meditation or enhance your current routine by centering your attention on an inspiring passage. One meditation practice that involves focusing on a passage is called "Lectio Divina," a traditional Christian contemplative practice. Here's how you can do it:

1. **Choose a Sacred Text or Inspirational Passage:** Select a passage from a sacred text or any inspirational writing. It could be a poem, quote, or piece of wisdom that resonates with you. I like to use affirmations, as the more you practice this particular meditation, the more the passage you use will be ingrained into your subconscious mind. I have shared one of my favourites, although if you decide to use it, feel free to change it to fit your preferences. We become what we constantly think about, so make your quote/affirmation as specific as you desire. *"I am a source of strength and positivity. Each day, I embrace challenges with resilience and learn*

valuable lessons. My journey is a canvas, and I paint it with gratitude and joy.
I am capable, deserving, and destined for success. Today, I choose to radiate
love and kindness, making a positive impact on myself and those around me."

2. **Prepare Your Space:** Try to set aside the same time of day, where it is a quiet and comfortable place to sit. I make space to complete my meditation in the morning, so I am ready start my day feeling at peace. Ensure that you won't be disturbed during your meditation and commit to making it your ritual. I usually set side around twenty-five minutes if time permits, but to start, maybe give yourself five minutes, and build your way up, in increments of five minutes, until you get to your desired timeframe.

3. **Relax and Breathe:** While in a sitting position, close your eyes, take a few deep breaths, and allow yourself to relax. Focus on your breath to centre your mind.

4. **Read Aloud:** Read the chosen passage slowly and aloud. Pay attention to each word and let the words sink in. Repeat the reading a few times, until you cherish the meaning. Visualize the passage, feel the passage, be at one with the passage.

5. **Reflect:** Close your eyes and reflect on the words. Consider their significance in your life. Allow any thoughts or emotions to arise without judgment.

6. **Meditate:** Let go of the words and sit in silent meditation. Focus on your breath or the sensations in your body. If your mind wanders, gently bring it back to the passage. It is important that you do not condemn yourself if your mind starts to wonder.

7. **Contemplate:** As you end your meditation, contemplate how the passage can guide your thoughts and actions throughout the day. Make a note of your thoughts and feelings in your Renaissance notebook.

This practice helps cultivate mindfulness, reflection, and a deeper connection with the chosen passage. Keep in mind that you can adapt this practice to suit your personal beliefs and preferences.

Transcendental Meditation (TM)

Katie Compton, a successful serial entrepreneur, found solace and balance in the bustling world of business through Transcendental Meditation (TM). Amid the demands of her thriving career, Katie felt the need to cultivate a sense of inner calm and clarity. She was a devout Christian and one day while studying the bible, she came across the word Maranatha, an Aramaic word that meant "Our Lord, come!"

Katie would repeat this specific word, to guide her mind into a state of relaxed awareness. For Katie, this practice became a sanctuary, allowing her to disconnect from the chaotic external world and delve into the serene depths of her consciousness.

One of the reasons Katie gravitated toward TM was its simplicity. The effortless nature of silently repeating the mantra 'ma-rah-natha, made it accessible for her busy lifestyle. It became a daily ritual, a pause button amid the constant demands, offering a profound sense of stillness.

As Katie delved deeper into TM, she discovered a myriad of benefits. The regular practice not only alleviated stress but also enhanced her focus and creativity. She found herself approaching challenges with a newfound resilience and a clearer perspective. The soothing effects of TM spilled over into her daily life, fostering better relationships and a heightened sense of well-being.

TM had become an integral part of her success story, demonstrating that amidst the whirlwind of a bustling career, you can find tranquillity through the power of meditation.

Guidance for Your Contemplative Exercises

When initiating reflective practices, consider recording your intention in your Renaissance journal and aim for a commitment of sixty-six days, the duration needed to establish a habit. Have faith in the process, subsequently reflecting on your experience to determine if the results were positive enough to warrant continued engagement or if another practice might be more suitable.

Managing Boundary Violations

As you delve into your contemplative journey, you'll attune yourself to the attitudes and expectations of those around you. Renaissance philosophers revered time as a divine gift, meant for both personal use and sharing. If someone insists on your time as if it's a debt owed, recognize them as a boundary violator attempting to exert control. Resist and stay true to your path, following your heart and focusing on your ultimate end goal. During meditation, you may confront restlessness, boredom, or even fears and doubts—emotions that have always lingered beneath the surface. If you are dealing with profound fear, anxiety, or depression, seek professional support. For the routine mental clutter, persist with the meditation techniques provided earlier or consider meditation audio for continued mental clarity. Sometimes I use Rockstar Affirmations, as my meditation audio, while working, or just before I go to bed. You can find their large collection of affirmations on YouTube, which I highly recommend. https://www.youtube.com/c/RockstarAffirmations

No Man Is an Island

Psychologists say that we need a healthy community, to support a healthy sense of self. In this section of key six, we will explore the importance of having the right support system, so you can live out your masterpiece.

Every person from the Renaissance, did not live out their purpose by themselves. They drew inspiration from role models, mentors, and nurturing friendships. Young individuals acquired their skills either through parental guidance or by joining the workforce during their teenage years. At times, they even lived with their mentors, gaining valuable skills, instilling crucial values, and assuming responsibilities of adulthood.

Apprenticeships typically spanned seven years, and upon completion, many progressed to higher positions. In comparison, our contemporary society is characterized by a rapid pace and compartmentalization. Most young people in the Western world have limited exposure to the world of work, dedicating the majority of their time to peers—approximately thirty-five hours a week during school. To embrace our callings as contemporary renaissance individuals, we must foster mentoring communities that cultivate supportive relationships, aiding us in fulfilling our purpose.

Mentors can assist you in various ways, such as providing guidance, sharing knowledge and expertise, offering support, and helping you navigate challenges. They play a crucial role in personal and professional development by providing valuable insights and encouragement. They can help you believe in yourself, enough for you to achieve the impossible.

Don't believe me? Well according to the Pygmalion effect, (also known as the Rosenthal effect), it is a psychological phenomenon where higher expectations lead to an increase in performance. The term originated from a study conducted by psychologists Robert Rosenthal and Lenore Jacobson in 1968. In their study, teachers were told that certain students were identified as "academic bloomers" based on a false classification. These students, however, showed significant intellectual gains compared to their peers. The Pygmalion effect suggests that when others have positive expectations about an individual's abilities, it can influence that person to perform better. This phenomenon highlights the impact of expectations and the self-fulfilling nature of positive beliefs.[19]

Tristan experienced this first hand. He grew up in the United Kingdom, where he was in the gifted class for all of his lessons. At the age of eight, Tristan moved to New York, with his parents. He settled into life very quickly and seemed to be doing well, until they discovered that he was failing in his math class. The approach to mathematics in New York students varied significantly from that in London, however it had been Tristan's favourite topic, and now it felt as if it was fast becoming his least.

As time went by, he got slightly better at math, however he then relocated to California. He soon discovered that in Los Angeles, math was done in a completely different way than New York and London. Tristan had lost all hope, and he dreaded going to math class. The love he once had for math, had dissipated, and he would constantly put himself down. Tristan's parents disliked seeing their young champion feel so defeated, and so they decided to get a mentor for him. They found Brad, a math tutor, who had a heart for young people.

After three months of weekly sessions with Tristan, Brad had boosted Tristan's confidence in math, and by the conclusion of the school year, Tristan emerged as the top student in his class. Tristan became independent of Brad's assistance, yet Brad would forever hold a special place in Tristan's heart. Brad not only restored Tristan's confidence in math but also instilled a sense of invincibility across all his studies. Ultimately, Tristan even skipped a grade in school.

Knowing When to Leave

Just as we observed the positive impact of mentors, the inverse could also hold true. Recognizing when you've surpassed a mentorship is crucial. While mentors provide valuable knowledge, there comes a time to move forward, just as Tristan experienced. Depending too heavily on mentors can hinder our ability to navigate independently. To help us know when it is time to move on from our mentors, ask yourself;

- ➢ Have I absorbed all the lessons I can from this person?
- ➢ Do I sense constraints, feeling unable to express myself authentically?
- ➢ Is it time to move on, and be independent?

When you know it is time to part ways from your mentor, use your communication skills you learnt earlier, and show them your gratitude for all they have done for you. There is nothing wrong with staying in touch, but not as an apprentice. It's time to spread your wings and fly.

Create a Renaissance Community

If you don't currently have a mentor, you should think about getting one. To find a mentor, look at the questions you answered in the previously, and think of someone who you admire. If you cannot be physically mentored by them, is there someone else in your community you can reach out to? Take positive action in reaching out.

Also be a mentor to yourself. How you may ask, you can say affirmations to yourself in the mirror, you can build on your relationship with yourself, be observant when you talk to yourself. Are you being kind to yourself? I like to use the following passage from the bible, to evaluate if I am being compassionate enough with myself;

"Love is patient and kind; love does not envy or boast; it is not arrogant or rude."

Another way to help yourself, is by helping someone else. As you share, without sacrificing your talent, you will receive more, more joy, more peace, more gifts.

Discerning Unhealthy & Toxic People

Evolving beyond a mentorship is a natural progression, but certain relationships can be toxic, undermining your dreams and inducing shame. Unless you're a certified counsellor, attempting to unravel these dynamics is unproductive. It's crucial to identify toxic relationships and maintain distance. Distinguishing between constructive criticism, which aids improvement, and toxic criticism, which demoralizes, is vital.

Engaging with such personalities is futile; befriending or satisfying them is also virtually impossible. The best course of action is to identify and avoid them at all costs to shield yourself from further harm. New Renaissance individuals promote each other's creative growth, and those hindering your life's purpose are not true friends. Toxic individuals often target those they perceive as 'different.' Meaningful relationships significantly impact our lives, and you deserve a Renaissance community that encourages a healthy and fulfilling life. Settle for nothing less.

So how do you identify these awful humans? While they may initially seem friendly, they sporadically deliver toxic criticism. They seldom listen, often talking over you and displaying irrational behaviour. They exhibit bias against you, avoiding celebration of your successes by diverting the conversation or making comparisons. Additionally, they consistently attempt to undermine you, aiming to sabotage your efforts. If you find one, run like your life depends on it.

Cultivate Your Friendships

Appreciate your friendships; never underestimate their value. Take time to acknowledge and celebrate friends who support, share common goals, and contribute to your creative growth. Regularly express your gratitude to them. They will surely cherish the recognition of your friendship.

⇒ Key Six Reflection Exercise ⇐

Take a few minutes to reflect on your progress in the first half of key six. You have nearly finished unlocking your peace, while making your life resemble a piece of art. In your Renaissance notebook, write your answers to the following prompts;

1. How have you found your contemplative practice has helped you?
2. Have you had to simplify your life to create space for your reflection time?

3. Have you been using a mantra? If not, choose one and begin using it, while noting your thoughts and feelings.

4. Have you taken the time to cultivate your own Renaissance community?

5. Have you found a mentor, who can help you in this season? If so, why did you choose them? If not, what three steps can you take this week, to try and find one?

6. Have you been a good friend recently, and if so, how?

7. Have you spent time with your friend group this week? If not, reach out to a friend today.

8. Have you remembered to share your knowledge, through mentoring someone else recently? If not, what two steps can you take this week, to become a mentor to someone?

9. What was your success highlight in this chapter and how did you celebrate?

Let's Get Creative

I intentionally saved creativity for the climax of key six. Ever strolled by a construction site and marvelled at how it seems to take an eternity for the builders to lay the foundation? Months pass, and suddenly, voila! A towering structure emerges seemingly out of nowhere. Now, think of the rest of this chapter as the concluding touch to laying the groundwork for your personal Renaissance. As you venture into the seventh and final key in the next chapter, visualize your ascent mirroring the speed of adept builders on a meticulously laid foundation.

Before we dive in, let me elaborate on the significance of groundwork in construction. The foundation stage is, pun intended, foundational to the entire process, providing crucial support to the structure. Your journey in this book has mirrored this meticulous approach.

With the foundation set, subsequent phases proceed with heightened efficiency. The stability from a well-constructed foundation propels rapid progress in erecting the superstructure. Everything now unlocked, you're poised to expedite your goals. Methodical planning and preparation pave the way for a smooth construction process, minimizing uncertainties and bolstering predictability and speed. As you transition into the final phase in key seven, trust that what you've built, you're well-equipped to sustain. So, with that, let's unleash our creativity!

A Work of Art

Creativity, a hallmark of the Renaissance, transformed the way we perceive ourselves and the world through figures like William Shakespeare. During this era, life was viewed as a masterpiece by Renaissance philosophers, inspiring creative pursuits across Western Europe. In England, Queen Elizabeth indulged in poetry, musical instruments, and dance, while households of farmers, merchants, and craftsmen embraced music after meals. Renaissance men and women excelled in writing, drawing, and music. Across ages, the connection endures, illustrating that art and beauty can enhance health and harmony in modern life. Let's cultivate your unique creative practice.

131

The Renaissance's admiration for the arts finds support in contemporary psychology, where researchers affirm that engaging in a creative practice can significantly enhance health and enrich one's life with greater meaning. Abraham Maslow linked creativity to being "healthy, self-actualizing, fully human,"[20] while positive psychologists consider it a crucial character strength. Studies demonstrate that adopting a creative practice not only fosters essential skills in young individuals but also helps adults maintain a sense of purpose.

Your creative endeavour aims to infuse more beauty into your life and can provide enhanced clarity as you pursue your calling. Whether it involves writing poetry, painting, dancing, singing, or playing music, your creative practice holds the potential for greater personal fulfilment.

Interpreting our experiences through the lens of music, poetry, drama, dance, and the visual arts allows you to perceive your life as organized patterns, akin to the harmonious structure of a symphony. The presence of harmony in our surroundings fosters inner harmony. Much like Maslow's hierarchy of needs emphasizes how an orderly home can uplift a person beyond poverty and adversity, leading to a healthy and productive life.[20]

Creativity introduces fresh harmonies and novel possibilities. When we create, we blend our individual talents with an indescribable force, shaping them into art. The trajectory and reach of our work remain unknown. In 2017, my move to Los Angeles marked one of the most challenging years of my life, filled with unforeseen events beyond my control. Amidst the chaos, I found comfort in the beauty around me. Nestled along the Pacific

Coast Highway, my home opened onto the tranquil stretch of Santa Monica beach. A regular ritual emerged – I'd stroll downstairs, go through garden, so I could feel the sand beneath my toes, and immerse myself in studying the original Hebraic calendar, a source of ancient wisdom with timeless relevance.

Lost in these discoveries, I sensed a compelling urge to share the profound insights that brought me hope during my personal trials. This moment sparked the birth of my podcast and YouTube channel. The response was remarkable – within a few weeks, my subscriber count soared past eleven thousand. Messages poured in, recounting how the shared information had become a beacon of transformation in people's lives. One caller, moved to tears, expressed gratitude for the bi-monthly podcast that instilled hope in her future.

Unexpectedly, my endeavours gained momentum, leading to invitations from YouTube for exclusive events at their Mar Vista headquarters, designed for their top creators. The journey from a personal hobby to a transformative platform was an unforeseen success, underscoring the profound impact that sharing our passions can have on the broader world.

Your own creative power can transform your life and your world in remarkable ways. Take a moment now to create your beauty practice.

⇒ Key Six Creative Beauty Exercise ⇐

Let's look at ways to create more conscious beauty in your life. I find beauty when I go hiking in the Palisades, or when I sit on my balcony every morning, with my hot lemon water, closely watching and listening to the hummingbirds, that come close to my ledge. Sometimes beauty can be taking a bath, with fresh rosemary and Epsom salts, listening to your favourite playlist, or burning an incense stick while fixating on a specific affirmation. For the next seven days, ask yourself daily;

➢ How can I find and create more beauty in my life each day?" If you're struggling in this area, ask yourself, what creative activities did you enjoy when you were a child. Did you enjoy sports, ceramics, knitting, role play? Many people today still benefit from the influence of engaging in play.

➢ Choose an activity and commit to engaging each day, then write in your Renaissance notebook how it made you feel.

➢ Could any areas of your life use more harmony?

➢ What steps can I take to create beauty and harmony in my life today?

As you cultivate increased creativity in your life, you engage in a transformative journey that extends beyond the grasp of your mind and the scope of your vision. The renaissance unfolding within you invariably sparks a renewal in your environment, opening up fresh opportunities for positively modifying our world.

PART III

Key Seven | The Commitment to Making Your Wildest Dreams Come True

Your time is limited, so don't waste it living someone else's life.

Steve Jobs

Congratulations, you've successfully reached the ultimate milestone.

Through unlocking new interests, discovering your authentic values, embracing joys and talents, crafting enriching experiences, and courageously taking creative strides, you've paved the way for your personal Renaissance. Now, let's explore strategies to sustain the liberation of your spirit and nurture ongoing personal growth.

A good way to do this is by using the skills you're utilizing right now: reading and reflecting. During the Renaissance, reading sparked a revolution in consciousness—an effect that, in contrast to our present

136

attitude, is often taken for granted today. The advent of the printing press in the 1400s marked a pivotal moment, democratizing access to written material. As a result, a multitude of individuals started engaging with written works, fostering independent thought. For Renaissance philosophers, reading was a transformative journey towards moral development, while for Christians, it became a crucial element in the pursuit of salvation.

The profound impact of reading acted as a catalyst for dramatic changes, giving rise to the Reformation and sparked breakthrough in science, politics, and the arts. Engaging with written words opened doors to new realms of understanding and perspectives. When we read, our mind becomes a theatre for another person's thoughts, transporting the reader into diverse lives and alternate worlds. Reading helps unravel significant patterns in one's own life, contributing to personal growth and a deeper comprehension of the world. Your cognitive engagement, reasoning, concentration, and critical thinking skills are also improved when exposed to books.[21]

Engaging with literature has the power to reshape your life. While individuals often tend to follow the social and cultural paths set by their parents, books offer a gateway to transcend this norm by presenting visions of alternative worlds. Take Shakespeare, for instance – despite concluding his formal education at Stratford Grammar School, he would immerse himself in reading by candlelight after a hectic day in the London theatres. His focus on ancient Roman writers left a profound impact on him.[22]

Reading serves as a catalyst for personal transformation and can propel you into your own renaissance. By delving into the lives of diverse characters, like those encountered in this book, you gain insights and develop skills that open up new avenues in alignment with your life's purpose. Additionally, the act of reading prompts essential reflection, unveiling fresh perspectives about yourself and the recurring patterns in your life.

Reading is a delicate equilibrium, demanding that you simultaneously hold not only the current sentence but also earlier sentences and personal experiences in your mind, all interwoven in a complex cognitive dance. Achieving this requires the utilization of brain areas associated with working memory. Mastering these skills is crucial for maintaining your personal Renaissance.

Understanding Your Story Through Patterns

Reading plays a significant role in enhancing self-awareness, allowing you to unravel the intricate patterns woven into your life. When you reflect on your life's narrative, recurring themes emerge, providing a profound understanding. Psychologists suggest that we construct narratives to bring greater coherence to our experiences. Narrating your story can serve as a spiritual practice and a wellspring of inspiration. Amid life's myriad demands, discerning larger patterns may be challenging, yet by revisiting the past, you can reveal them. Can you recognise the patterns in Paige's story?

Paige grew up in a small town, in up-state New York. She discovered she had a fascination with the stories of others from an early age. Often found in the library, she would curl up in the window seat, occasionally taking breaks to watch people strolling by. Growing up in a tight-knit community, Paige naturally became the unofficial confidante for friends and cousins, forging a deep connection with community support and belonging.

As a teenager, Paige faced her share of challenges, witnessing her parents' frequent conflicts, predominantly instigated by her mother. Her dad would seize every opportunity to escape the turmoil with his favourite line, "soon be back." Also, enduring verbal and physical abuse from her Mum, the very person meant to protect her, Paige found solace in autobiographies at the library, discovering ways people coped and healed. The resilience she witnessed in others left an indelible mark on her heart.

In high school, Paige's magnetism became apparent as she worked at a summer camp, drawing teens not just for help and advice but also for laughter and joy. Known for energizing those around her, Paige was always surrounded blots of people. She volunteered with a youth project aiding displaced young people, fostering a sense of community, and belonging. Recognizing her passion, the organizers invited her to speak at prestigious events, paving the way for her to take a psychology course in college.

Post-graduation, Paige pursued a career in therapy, enrolling in a counselling program to delve into the complexities of human behaviour. Her journey mirrored the challenges she observed in others, leading to moments of self-discovery and lessons in empathy and compassion.

A defining moment occurred when Paige nearly lost a close friend to mental health struggles and domestic violence, fuelling her commitment to help others navigate their challenges. Channelling grief into understanding the human condition, Paige became an award-winning public speaker, raising awareness about mental health and later expanding to address domestic violence. Her advocacy work became a powerful expression of her commitment to social impact.

Throughout her life, Paige maintained a commitment to education and lifelong learning, stemming from her early days in the library. Creative expression played a crucial role, evident in her part-time job, volunteering, and public speaking engagements. Nature and outdoor activities, particularly her time at the summer camp, served as sources of solace and inspiration.

Community connection remained a consistent theme, shaping Paige's ability to relate to diverse stories and experiences. Mentorship played a pivotal role, with significant figures guiding her choices and supporting her along the way. Cultural and spiritual influences also played a role in shaping Paige's understanding of human behaviour and healing.

Looking back over the course of her life, Paige marvelled at the intricate patterns that led her to become a renowned therapist and dynamic public speaker. Each chapter, filled with joy or sorrow, contributed to her ability to relate to the diverse stories that crossed her path, seeking healing.

Paige didn't choose a career; she discovered her purpose — the art of understanding and healing through shared stories. Some of Paige's personal themes were, discovery, adventure, community connection, creativity, nature, and cultural/spiritual influences. Now I'm inviting you to explore your patterns and themes.

⇒ Key Seven Sharing Your Story Exercise ⇐

Allocate approximately an hour in a quiet, undisturbed space with your Renaissance journaling. Take a few deep breathes and relax. Think back to when you were a child and try and answer the following questions:

1. What did you love to do as a child?
2. Did you have a favourite place to visit?
3. Who was the most special person in your life, and why?
4. Did your family function harmoniously, or did it face dysfunction? If the latter, what challenges and blessings did it present to you?
5. What was the most noteworthy event in your childhood?
6. Did a pivotal moment alter your perspective on life?
7. Was there something you were really proud of? If so, why did it make you proud?

Once you have recording at least two core memories for each question, read over your answers and make a note of any recurring patterns. Make a note of how your themes connect to your current calling/purpose? Understanding your personal theme enhances your discernment, which helps you make wiser choices throughout your ongoing Renaissance.

Shifting the Perspective of Your Story

At times, exercises may bring up past mistakes or shaming experiences, causing negative feelings about oneself. However, through reflection and subsequently reshaping these experiences, you can transition towards a more positive future. One common NLP technique for reframing negative experiences is called the "Swish Pattern." Here's a simplified version of the exercise:

- **Identify the Negative Image:** Close your eyes and vividly bring to mind the negative experience or image from your past. Make the image as clear and detailed as possible.

- **Create a Positive Replacement Image:** Now, imagine a small, distant, black-and-white image representing a positive outcome or a more empowering perspective related to the negative experience. Keep this image small and in the distance.

- **Get Ready to Swish:** Mentally create a large, bright, and colourful positive image that's more compelling and enjoyable than the negative one. Imagine this image like a tiny dot in the centre of your negative image.

- **Swish the Images:** In your mind, rapidly "swish" the two images. Visualize the small, negative image being rapidly replaced by the large, positive one. Make it like a quick, positive explosion that covers and replaces the negative image entirely.

- **Repeat:** Do this swishing process several times, making the positive image more vibrant and compelling each time.

- **Test:** After several swishes, test how you feel when you recall the initial negative experience. If the negative feelings have diminished or transformed into positive ones, you've successfully reframed the experience.

This exercise really helps my clients shift the way their mind associates with past negative experiences, creating a more positive and empowering perspective. You will be able to see the light beyond the darkness, living a personal Renaissance of grace and renewal. I know from experience, if you put this exercise in repetition, you will have the same results. It's really important to practice this exercise with an open mind and be patient with the process. Remember to always be gentle with yourself.

Let's take a moment to reflect on how far you have come. When we take the time to read and reflect, we unveil unexplored realms within and around us. Observing the narrative of your life unfold, you step forward as a revitalized Renaissance individual.

Physical Exercise Helps Your Journey

What is the extent of your weekly physical activity? Do you engage in activities like climbing stairs, hiking, going to the gym, playing sports, or practicing Pilates? In this day and age, it's common for individuals not to have a regular exercise routine. But according to many studies, including one recently, most people who don't have an exercise practice suffer with depression, anxiety, low self-esteem, low self-efficacy, and not much social support.[23] These symptoms are not the best way to sustain you on your Renaissance journey, as you will feel drained in no time. But there is a way to guard against inertia wiping out your energy and pulling you away from your dreams. Fostering a consistent exercise routine can amplify your strength and stamina, propelling you forward, and/or sustaining you in your personal Renaissance. Research indicates that regular exercise boosts vitality, motivation, and opens pathways to creative insights.

Physical activities came naturally to men and women in the Renaissance. In a society predominantly focused on agriculture, individuals dedicated their days to manual labour, such as tending to farms or journeying to markets to trade dairy products. In the absence of cars, mobiles, laptops, and drones, our counterparts during the renaissance covered considerable distances for daily tasks and social visits. Contemporary families predominantly rely on microwaves for cooking and cars for transportation, whereas in Renaissance days they engaged in active pursuits like hunting, and horse riding.

The widespread presence of modern technology has progressively diminished regular exercise in our daily routines. Convenience has ushered in a persistent deficiency of physical activity, but let's explore strategies to enhance your health and energy, cultivate your Renaissance journey and sustaining it over time.

⇒ Key Seven Enhancing Your Wellness Exercise ⇐

Health psychologists see wellness as a combination of physical, mental, and emotional health. When you exercise regularly, you take part in all three. It helps with you falling asleep faster, eradicates insomnia, reduces high blood pressure, reduces heart disease and diabetes, along with many other practical benefits. Exercise also stimulates your brain, which promotes better cognitive function and memory. Below are some useful tips to help you enhance your energy through exercise. For the next seven days, commit to taking action and make a note of what you done and how you felt in your Renaissance notebook.

- **Create a Consistent Routine:** Establish a regular exercise schedule that fits into your daily routine, aim for a balance between frequency and intensity.

- **Choose Activities You Enjoy:** Select exercises that you find enjoyable to increase long-term adherence. Whether it's dancing, hiking, cycling, or team sports, make it fun. Start off with a small amount of time, maybe 20-30 minutes, and then gradually increase the intensity and duration of your workouts as your fitness level improves.

- **Stay Active Throughout the Day:** Incorporate incidental physical activity, like taking the stairs, walking during breaks, or doing quick stretches.

- **Prioritize Recovery:** Allow time for rest and recovery between intense workouts to prevent burnout and reduce the risk of injuries. You can incorporate activities like foam rolling, stretching, and adequate sleep to support recovery.

- **Track Your Progress:** Monitor your fitness progress, make notes on your new exercise practice in your Renaissance notebook, and celebrate your successes to stay motivated and committed to your exercise routine.

While it may appear as a minor step, it holds monumental significance. Your workouts have the potential to enhance your life, often in ways you might never anticipate. Carrie, who found herself fully immersed in the demanding world of a high-end restaurant, where the stress of managing customer expectations and fast-paced service took a toll on her well-being. Long hours and constant pressure left her physically and emotionally drained. One day, a caring friend noticed Carrie's struggles and suggested something unconventional yet transformative – a Pilates class. Sceptical at first, Carrie decided to give it a try, seeking an escape from the stress that consumed her daily life.

As she stepped into the serene Pilates studio, the atmosphere immediately contrasted with the chaos of her restaurant job. Guided by a skilled instructor, Carrie embraced the movements that engaged her body and mind. With each session, she discovered a sense of control and focus that served as a respite from the chaotic restaurant environment. To Carrie's surprise, the impact was not just physical. As she committed to her Pilates practice, the stress that once weighed heavily on her shoulders began to dissipate. Her body felt stronger and looked more toned, an unexpected bonus that fuelled her motivation to continue.

Encouraged by the positive changes in her life, Carrie made a bold decision – she would train to become a Pilates teacher herself. The prospect of sharing the transformative power of Pilates with others excited her, offering a new direction for her career.

The regular Pilates sessions not only sculpted Carrie's physique but also had a profound effect on her mental well-being. The release of endorphins during exercise became her natural mood booster, bringing about a sense of peace and tranquillity she hadn't experienced in years.

As the stress melted away, so did Carrie's fatigue, transforming her once exhausting routine into a manageable and even enjoyable experience.

Carrie's journey from a stressed restaurant worker to a vibrant and energized Pilates teacher showcased the incredible impact that holistic well-being can have on one's life. The decision to step into that Pilates class not only sculpted her body but also sculpted a new path filled with peace, energy, and a renewed sense of purpose.

As Carrie discovered, your exercise practice can help you move forward on many levels, beyond what you could fathom.

Disclaimer Consult with a healthcare professional or fitness expert before starting a new exercise program, especially if you have pre-existing health conditions. Listen to your body, and always stay hydrated.

Why You Need Boundaries

Boundaries are the personal limits and guidelines we establish to define acceptable behaviour, interactions, and experiences in our lives. They serve as the invisible fences that protect our well-being, ensuring that we maintain alignment with our core values and goals. These boundaries act as safeguards, helping us navigate relationships, work, and various aspects of life while preserving our mental, emotional, and physical health.

Establishing boundaries is crucial because they create a framework that delineates what is acceptable and unacceptable in our interactions with others and ourselves. By clearly defining these limits, we communicate our needs, expectations, and values to those around us. This clarity not only fosters healthy relationships but also acts as a compass, guiding us toward choices and situations that align with our personal values and aspirations, and helps us sustain them. Kevin and Abby learnt that the hard way, finding themselves entangled in the complexities of running a business together. They were a dynamic couple, united not just by love but by a shared vision of creating something meaningful. Little did they know that their lack of boundaries would soon jeopardize not only their company but also their relationship.

At the outset, everything seemed promising. They were enthusiastic, passionate, and deeply invested in their joint venture. However, as the business grew, so did the demands on their time and energy. Kevin, the visionary, often found himself absorbed in work late into the night, while Abby, the detail-oriented executor, was tirelessly managing day-to-day operations.

The boundaries between work and personal life blurred gradually. Dinner conversations morphed into business meetings, and weekends meant catching up on pending tasks rather than relaxation. Their home became an extension of the office, and the once vibrant relationship started to fray under the weight of constant work-related stress.

One critical turning point came when they found themselves in a heated argument during what was supposed to be a weekend getaway. The lines between discussing business strategies and personal grievances had vanished, leaving them emotionally drained and questioning the future of both their company and their relationship.

One day, their close friend Hannah, realised the urgency of the situation, while they were all together at the pub one weekend. A simple conversation that turned into work politics, mixed with aggression. They needed to implement clear and specific boundaries, asap. With the help of their long-time friend, first and foremost, they designated certain areas in their home as "work-free zones" to reclaim personal space. They set defined working hours, respecting each other's need for dedicated time away from the business.

Additionally, Kevin and Abby established a rule: no business discussions during meals, which was the reason Hannah even noticed the urgency of installing boundaries in their relationship. This simple yet powerful boundary allowed them to reconnect on a personal level, fostering a healthier balance between their professional and personal lives.

They also recognized the importance of regular check-ins to discuss both business and relationship matters. These intentional conversations ensured that concerns were addressed promptly, preventing small issues from snowballing into major conflicts.

Implementing these boundaries wasn't without its challenges. It required discipline, communication, and a shared commitment to make their business thrive while preserving their relationship. Slowly but surely, the impact of these boundaries became evident, to the point their friends were noticing the difference.

The once strained atmosphere began to lift. With designated work hours, they were more focused and efficient during the day, reducing the need for late-night work sessions. Their home regained its warmth as they learned to compartmentalize work and personal life.

Kevin and Abby's journey serves as a testament to the transformative power of boundaries. By drawing clear lines between their professional and personal spheres, they not only salvaged their business but also reignited the flame of their relationship. The company thrived, their friendships benefited and more importantly, so did their love story, proving that in the delicate dance of business and romance, boundaries are the choreography that ensures harmony.

Just as Kevin and Abby experienced, many challenges emerge when we neglect to establish and uphold effective boundaries. When we lack clarity on our responsibilities and fail to differentiate between what we are accountable for and what we are not, various negative symptoms manifest. These symptoms serve as indicators of an underlying issue. Individuals who come to me, seeking therapy, often present with the symptoms we're about to delve into, but the root problem frequently lies in the confusion surrounding the establishment and management of boundaries.

Signs of Neglecting to Set Boundaries

Numerous individuals encounter depression due to a failure in establishing healthy boundaries. The absence of clear boundaries exposes them to mistreatment, resulting in significant pain. Others struggle with depression by internalizing anger directed at those who apply control over them. This occurs when they are unaware of their free will and allow others to dictate their choices. The consequence is often a sense of resentment, possibly even bitterness. Other indicators of a lack of boundaries are;

- Impulsivity
- Feelings of Being Let Down
- Isolation
- Masochism
- Procrastination
- Impulsivity
- Obsessive-Compulsive Behaviour
- Panic

- Resentment
- Co-dependency
- Passive-Aggressive Behaviour
- Identity Confusion
- Blaming
- Victim Mentality
- Under Responsibility
- Generalized Anxiety
- Difficult Being Alone

Be honest, and write down in your Renaissance notebook if you acknowledge experiencing any of these symptoms, and find a correlation to instances where boundaries were absent?

Learning to Implement Boundaries

Despite our efforts, there are times when we let people breach our boundaries due to the barriers we create from past injuries and distortions. One of the major challenges in boundary work is overcoming the guilt associated with claiming the freedom to control our own lives. Many individuals have been conditioned to believe that placing their feelings, behaviours, and choices is selfish or wrong, creating co-dependent patterns. For people with low self-esteem, their needs often take a backseat as they prioritize others' responses. However, it is crucial to build a robust "NO" muscle, a skill learned in childhood for setting boundaries. Unfortunately, many of us have phased out this word from our vocabulary and must rediscover its importance. Learning to assertively say no, particularly to those close to us, is arguably the most vital yet challenging aspect of establishing effective boundaries.

Having well-defined boundaries contributes to a sense of empowerment, allowing us to stay true to our life values and goals.

In essence, boundaries are essential tools for maintaining a healthy balance in our lives. They help us cultivate authenticity, foster positive connections, and navigate life's challenges with resilience and integrity, all the qualities you need help you sustain you on your Renaissance journey.

Discipline & Dedication

In the course of this book, you've cultivated your talents, uncovering your Renaissance, incorporating one practice at a time to aid you on your path. Now, you're poised for the ultimate practice – discipline and dedication. This practice, building upon the others, empowers you to manifest your dreams into reality.

Numerous individuals embark on a personal growth journey with initial enthusiasm, yet a considerable number abandon their aspirations before reaching their goals. The absence of discipline and dedication causes their visions for a better life to gradually decline. However, by maintaining consistent effort directed towards your dreams, the pathway to a new life unfolds. The essential elements lie in perseverance, continuous practice, and an unwavering faith in your dreams. Discipline and dedication have been consistent features in the lives of achievers throughout history, enabling them to turn their aspirations into tangible reality.

The crucial element is to persist, engage in regular practice, and maintain faith in your dreams. Throughout history, discipline and dedication have been the defining features in the lives of achievers, enabling many to turn their dreams into reality with these strengths. One notable example of someone who knew their dream, and persevered through her trials and tribulations is Marie Curie. From a young age, Marie displayed a keen interest in science and a dream of pursuing higher education despite societal norms of the time limiting women's access to education. She encountered financial hardships, scepticism, and criticism from some in the scientific community, and her affair with physicist Paul Langevin further subjected her to public scrutiny. Despite these overwhelming challenges, Curie persevered, continuing her ground-breaking scientific research. and becoming the first female professor at the University of Paris. Her unwavering dedication to her scientific pursuits also led her to become the first woman to win a Nobel Prize and the only person to win Nobel Prizes in two different scientific fields (physics and chemistry).

As you've progressed through the program outlined in this book, you've identified the obstacles hindering your path to achieving your dream. The following pages will assist you in cultivating a sustaining discipline to further support your journey.

Research in neuroscience has revealed that engaging in disciplined practice creates new neural connections, effectively priming your mind for moments of creative insight.[24] Neuroscientists have also discovered that during adolescence, the activities we engage in play a crucial role in shaping the neural connections that persist into adulthood. Immersing ourselves in daily rituals with care, commitment, and focused attention fosters inner strength, providing a deeper sense of meaning in life. This not only promotes healthy personal development but also lays the foundation for future success. Without these strengths, individuals may find it challenging to reach their goals. Kobe Bryant practiced these strengths from a young age, he would spend numerous hours honing his basketball skills. He started playing basketball when he was three, and the Lakers were his favourite team when he was growing up. When he was six, his father retired from the NBA and moved his family to Italy to continue playing professional basketball. Kobe began to play basketball seriously while living in Reggio Emilia and his grandfather would mail him videos of NBA games for him to study.[25]

It's reported that he adhered to a strict workout and diet regimen. He would work out for 6 months, 6 days a week, for at least 6 hours a day.

Kobe Bryant became one of the most successful basketball players of all–time. The winner of 5 NBA championships and 2 Olympic Gold Medals, amassing a net worth of more than $200 million during his playing career, proving that engaging wholeheartedly in our actions, approaching life's daily rituals with care, commitment, and concentrated attention, fosters inner strength and unveils deeper meaning in our lives. Discipline and dedication are the building blocks of success in any domain and when people find their lives purpose, their work comes from a place of passion, not obligation and brings them true happiness.

Modern Day Dedication

In the midst of modern distractions, maintaining dedication can be challenging. Dedication manifests in various ways—persisting through challenges, adapting to change, facing personal tragedies, navigating political upheavals, and more. From the Renaissance to the present day, creative individuals consistently demonstrate that perseverance, in the face of adversity, empowers us to achieve our dreams. James, a Chicago-born poet, faced adversity growing up on the south side. His journey included personal struggles, notably the impact of absent fatherhood explored in his poignant poem "Dear Father."[26] Through his art, he channelled these challenges into a powerful narrative of self-discovery and resilience.

For decades, James persevered, writing, and reciting his poetry wherever he would be, while also using poetry to navigate the complexities of his life. His impactful spoken word performances eventually caught the attention of the music industry, leading to collaborations with Kanye West, Jay-Z, and others.

After years of dedication, his perseverance paid off when he won a Grammy Award for Best Spoken Word Album. This recognition marked a triumphant moment in his career, showcasing the enduring power of his work in addressing personal struggles and societal issues.

Your calling entails a daily routine aimed at cultivating your strengths. While it may not always provide immediate joy, navigating through challenges and adversity in this routine can spark fresh insights, which will help you build your faith.

Moving Forward in Power

Whether your calling leads you to art, music, science, political action, or any other pursuit, pursuing your goals and staying true to your values constitutes a Renaissance journey. This journey not only enriches your life with new blessings but also brings forth gifts that the world eagerly awaits. Someone somewhere is anticipating the unveiling of your unique contributions to the world.

Having ventured into the unknown, akin to many Renaissance explorers, as your Renaissance journey persists, continue advancing by upholding your established habits and practices. Regularly revisit the lessons in this book, document your progress, and always bear in mind that within you resides the promise of tomorrow – your distinctive gift to the world.

Embarking on your new Renaissance, embracing your calling, involves maintaining faith in your unique gifts and discerning the patterns within and around you. This principle has been acknowledged by numerous Renaissance and contemporary scholars, writers, and artists, as highlighted in this book. The enduring Renaissance belief in interconnectedness persists today, emphasizing the interconnected nature of everything in the world. Always remember the treasure of your own uniqueness, stay faithful to your gifts, facilitating navigation of your inner compass to follow your heart. Wishing you the very best on your ongoing Renaissance journey.

⇒ Key Seven Final Reminders ⇐

The choices you make today, affect your future. As you continue on your Renaissance journey, here are some reminders from your final key.

- ➤ Expand your world through reading
- ➤ Look for meaningful patterns in the story of your life
- ➤ Reframe your negative stories using your NLP exercise
- ➤ Make more active choices, and increase your strength by exercising
- ➤ Make sure you review, update, and stick to your boundaries
- ➤ Keep your momentum with your discipline and dedication
- ➤ Always follow what brings you joy and momentum
- ➤ Never hide your gifts and talents from the world
- ➤ Focus on your strengths, and not your weaknesses
- ➤ Small actions, amount to huge life changing results, if you stay the course

When embracing your authentic values and living with purpose will lead the world to unfold a myriad of opportunities to support you.

FINAL OVERVIEW

Once you have taken the time to sit still and review yourself internally, these valuable insights into your present mindset will make you well-prepared to navigate the path toward positive transformation. Here's how to direct your adventure effectively:

Goal setting emerges as a potent tool, permitting you to define clear, specific, and attainable goals. These should resonate with your deepest desires, igniting your passion and motivation.

Equally vital is the art of challenging self-limiting beliefs. Identify these thought patterns and, with resolve, replace them with affirmations and constructive thoughts that underpin your goals.

Cultivate a growth mindset. Embrace lifelong learning, seeking new knowledge, skills, and experiences. Your commitment to expanding your horizons becomes the vessel of your transformation.

Envision an environment that nurtures positivity and motivation. Pay attention to the company you keep, the content you consume, and the spaces you inhabit. These factors have a profound influence on your mindset.

Mindfulness and meditation serve as valuable allies. Through these practices, you become more attuned to your thoughts and emotions, gaining mastery over stress, and fostering a constructive mindset.

Self-care, in all its facets, becomes non-negotiable. Physical health, mental well-being, and emotional balance form the bedrock upon which your journey to a positive mindset is built.

A support system is essential. Engage with trusted friends, mentors, or coaches who can encourage and hold you accountable. Their presence is your tether to progress.

Remember, adaptability is a virtue. Stay open to change, recognizing that setbacks and failures are part of the journey. These are stepping stones to your growth.

A practice of gratitude is your passport to positivity. As you acknowledge your blessings, your focus naturally shifts toward the positive aspects of life, elevating your overall mindset. Even when you go through troubling times you must continue acknowledge how you feel but don't self-isolate. Try to continue the following;

- Write your current thoughts and feelings in your journal.
- Complete some and/or all of the exercises in this book to help you reflect.
- Pray, meditate and/or talk to God, your higher power.

- Reach out to trusted sources like a therapist, life coach etc.

- Get in tune with nature, go for a hike or the beach.

- Make sure you rest, eat well, and get lots of sleep.

In conclusion, the journey of assessing your current mindset and making positive shifts is not a finite expedition. Rather, it's a continuous odyssey, demanding patience, self-compassion, and unswerving dedication. By understanding where you currently stand and setting a course for positive change, you're taking the first strides toward a transformative and fulfilling life—a life that you design in accordance with your true self.

AFTERWORD

So, this is where I wanted to get personal with you about how this book came into fruition. Unknowingly I had been pregnant with this book for a very long time, and sometimes just as a pregnant woman can end up going past her due date, that is how I would describe the birth of this book. Nevertheless, the book came at the exact right time, and I wouldn't have had it any other way. I have been certified as an NLP practitioner for decades, and as a result I try to live and talk intentionally at all times. I have travelled millions of miles around the world, shared my advice on the vital skills I have shared in this book with numerous people from different cultures, beliefs, and backgrounds, but yet universally there are principles that regardless of these differences, seem to be the same.

There are times when I observe my behaviour and also times where I observe interactions between others, and one thing for certain is we can always do better. We have the ability to reinvent ourselves and have a rebirth, to live multiple times within this lifetime. After a considerable number of rebirths, I thought it was only right to disseminate my wisdom on a larger scale than the people I have already had the privilege of sharing with. I truly try to live out everything in this book, but let's keep it real, I'm human and I slip up from time to time. My misjudgements have helped shape this book, as every encounter helps us to help others. Sometimes I have found myself in situations where my skills have literally gone right out the window.

Example: One day I was at the gas station and the attendant was being very rude, while moving very slowly. I was in a rush, and if late to my destination I would incur a hefty fee. It was safe to say that I was not in the mood. I remember her last comment was enough for me, my tone was not the nicest and I paid, and left. I ended up being really late because of the actions of the gas station attendant, but because I was well known in the establishment I was attending, I did not incur a late fee. Later that evening while reviewing my day, it was clear to me that there was a different way I could have handled the situation. The next day I decided to call the gas station and thankfully the lady in question was present, so I was able to apologize to her. Why you may ask? Well, the ultimate goal in any given interaction is for us to always evaluate ourselves. If I was fully present that day, I would *not* have fed into her low vibrations.

The lesson in this is to be aware of our triggers, and when we see the early warning signs of behaviours within ourselves that we know lead us to negativity we need to make a conscious shift. When we catch ourselves early, we can eradicate problems early, but only when we're vigilant. There will be times when miss the mark, but guess what? You can redeem yourself by creating the healthy habits we need, and also work on how we communicate. When we allow ourselves to learn from our mistakes, we not only enrich and strengthen our lives, but can enrich and strengthen the people within our sphere of influence. We have to train our mindset like we train our muscles in the gym, through repetition, anything is possible when we focus on our personal transformation and not look to and point the finger at other people.

If you use everything set out in this book, in the exact way that it is intended you will see changes in yourself, it may not always be appreciated or reciprocated by those around you, however when you focus on self and your outcomes, your genuineness and respect for self will always outshine every situation. It's through these lessons of life that helped me to birth this book. I hope it has planted a seed or watered what was already blooming within you. Now go and share your gifts and be great within your world.

ENDNOTES

1. Klein Law Group Blog; Divorce Data 2023 (Insights exploring the latest trends in US divorce data). Read through Klein Attorney

2. McEwen and Wingfield, 2003 Can Stress at Work Affect Cognitive Performance Study. Read on Cambridge Cognition website.

3. Empress Dowager CIXI The Concubine Who Launched Modern China – Author Jung Chang (Published 2013)

4. Fredrickson BL. The role of positive emotions in positive psychology: The broaden-and-build theory of positive emotions. American Psychologist: Special Issue. 2001; 56: 218–226.

5. Quote from Chinese Philosopher Lao Tzu

6. For a psychological study of values and meaning today, see R. F. Baumeister, Meanings of Life (New York: Guildford 1991)

7. Aion — Researches into the Phenomenology of the Self, published by Carl Jung in 1969

8. Baumeister and Vohs (2002), studies of values, health, and well-being. "How to increase and sustain positive emotion: The effects of expressing gratitude and visualizing best possible selves." The journal of positive psychology 1 (2006): 73-82

9. Excellent Quotations for Home and School by Julia B. Hoitt, (page 51), 1888

10. Journal of the American Psychoanalytic Association: "Why people talk to themselves."

11. 2005 study by the National Science Foundation

12. Dean Ornish, Love and Survival: The Healing Power of Intimacy (Harper & Collins, 1998) pg. 54-56 & 63

13. The Conservation of Resources (COR) theory, proposed by Stevan E. Hobfoll in 1989

14. Peak Performance: Elevate Your Game, Avoid Burnout, and Thrive with the New Science of Success. Author: Stulberg B., Magness S. - Rodale Books; New York, NY, USA: 2017

15. Mindfulness and Emotion Regulation: Insights from Neurobiological and Psychological Studies National Center for Biotechnology Information - Article PMC4350240 https://www.ncbi.nlm.nih.gov/pmc/articles/PMC4350240/

16. A Cross-Sectional Study on the Relationship Between Meditation Training and Emotional Intelligence National Center for Biotechnology Information - Article PMC6510032 https://www.ncbi.nlm.nih.gov/pmc/articles/PMC6510032/

17. Mindfulness Meditation: A Research-Proven Way to Reduce Stress October 30, 2019, published on the American psychological association https://www.apa.org/topics/mindfulness/meditation

18. The Neuroscience of Mindfulness Meditation - Tang, YY., Hölzel, B. & Posner, M. The neuroscience of mindfulness meditation. Nat Rev Neurosci 16, 213–225 (2015). nature reviews neuroscience https://doi.org/10.1038/nrn3916

19. Self-Fulfilling Prophecy: A Practical Guide to Its Use in Education by Robert T. Tauber - Release Date February 1997, Bloomsbury Publishing PLC

20. Maslow, A. H. (1943). A theory of human motivation. Psychological Review, 50, 370–396 & Maslow, A. H. (1968). Toward a psychology of being. New York: Wiley.

21. Knowledge growth and maintenance across the life span: The role of print exposure. Developmental Psychology. Stanovich KE, West RF, Harrison MR. 1995; 31(5).811., What reading does for the mind. American Education Journal. Stanovich KE, Cunningham AE. 1998, The importance of deep reading. Challenging the Whole Child: Reflections on Best Practices in Learning, Teaching, and Leadership. Wolf M, Barzillai M, Dunne J. 2009;130.

22. The Life of William Shakespeare: A Critical Biography 1st Edition 2017, by Lois Potter, 1st edition (May 7, 2012)

23. Physical activity and depression: Towards understanding the antidepressant mechanisms of physical activity by Kandola A., Ashdown-Franks G., Hendrikse J., Sabiston C.M., Stubbs B. - Neurosci. Biobehav. Rev. 2019; 107:525–539.

24. Sawyer K. The cognitive neuroscience of creativity: A critical review. Creativity Research Journal. 2011;23(2):137-154. DOI: 10.1080/10400419.2011.571191

25. MacMullen, Jackie (June 4, 2010). Kobe Bryant: Imitating Greatness. ESPN.com.

26. Dear Father: Breaking the Cycle of Pain Hardcover – January 27, 2015 by J. Ivy

ABOUT THE AUTHOR

Meet the extraordinary Va'rai Unique, a brilliant serial entrepreneur, author, and a master of Neuro-Linguistic Programming (NLP). Her words on the page are as captivating as her ability to decode and influence the human mind. With an uncanny talent for storytelling and a deep understanding of NLP techniques, she crafts narratives that not only entertain but also empower, inspire, and always transforms all who come into contact with her. Va'rai Unique's combination of literary prowess and NLP expertise has the power to change lives and shape the future of personal development and literature. She is a true force to be reckoned with, leaving an indelible mark on both the literary world and the realm of human potential.

WANT TO GET BETTER?

<u>**Attend a Va'rai Unique webinar**</u>

Personal – Change Starts Within

Successfully solve any individual behaviours that might be holding you back at home or at work. Work on your interpersonal skills to foster open communication around emotional, high stakes and/or risky topics.

Corporate - Influence Shapes Within

Enhance leadership and accountability, improve your performance, and ensure execution. Through rapid and sustainable behaviour change for teams and even entire organizations.

ALSO FROM THE BESTSELLING AUTHOR

Playing Life to Win - Accountability Journal

Did you know that you can make you can make your wildest dreams come true? Well, I am here to tell you that the ability is there, but many do not know where to start. The 'PLAYING LIFE TO WIN' journal will help you achieve your biggest business and/or personal goals with the help of the exercises included in the journal.

With our accountability journal you will put actions over words and make every decision count. With my simple steps in this guided journal, you will learn how to focus on ideas that work, and how to get rid of anything that is a distraction from your ultimate goal.

This journal is for those who want the blueprint to their personal idea of success, playing life to win! You will enjoy some stories and exercises to keep you on track, this journal is the best investment that you've ever made.

Available for pre-order now https://varaiunique.com/shop/p/goal-journal.

www.ingramcontent.com/pod-product-compliance
Lightning Source LLC
Chambersburg PA
CBHW030248130626
46549CB00002B/439